Proof of Concept
Writing the Short Script

PROD. NO.
SCENE
DATE
PROD. CO.
DIRECTOR
CAMERAMAN

POP CORN

Juliet Giglio
Keith Giglio

Kendall Hunt
publishing company

Kendall Hunt
publishing company

www.kendallhunt.com
Send all inquiries to:
4050 Westmark Drive
Dubuque, IA 52004-1840

CONTENTS

CHAPTER 14   Proof of Concept Exercises **217**

PREFACE

WRITTEN BY YOU

The director waits for the great screenplay for their next movie to direct. The actor waits for the great television script that will resurrect their career and get them that Emmy nomination. The agent waits for that great screenplay they can send to the producer waiting for the screenplay, then send to the studio so they can make it and they can thrill a ticket-buying audience.

Where is that great screenplay? Where is that great television pilot?

You're writing it.

Maybe not today.

Maybe not tomorrow, but soon . . .

And for the rest of your lives . . .

THE SHORT SCRIPT—THE VISUAL RESUME

The short film has become the new spec script in Hollywood. Agents and producers spend part of their day not reading scripts, but watching films—short films that serve as a visual résumé. From Martin Scorsese, Steven Spielberg, Francis Ford Coppola, and George Lucas to Ava DuVernay to Jason Reitman, Wes Anderson, and Christopher Nolan, short films launched careers for these writers and directors.

It makes sense. Before the writer can run up to accept the Oscar, they need to learn to walk. This book is designed to teach you to walk. We will cover all the core principals of dramatic construction. From development of the idea to delivery of the script, you will learn that the same elements present in long-form narrative are the same as in a short film; how the characters' arcs in television shows that span seasons are the same in a short script; how short-form film structure is the same but different from long-form film structure.

Write a great short and you are started on your way to a long career. From there you can build on your skill and jump to longer form. Before he wrote *Dunkirk*, Christopher Nolan wrote and directed a short called *Doodlebug*. You're thinking, "I have never heard of *Doodlebug*"—you will.

We encourage writers to take directing classes to learn the production side. Scripts are written for movies to be made. There is nothing more powerful today than the hyphenate (i.e., the writer who can also produce or, even better, direct). You wrote the short script. No one knows it better than you. With amazing advances in technology, go out and film your shorts. Mark and Jay Duplass (unofficial kings of Sundance, independent film, and television comedies) started off by making a seven-minute film that cost three dollars. Yes, three dollars.[1] The Duffer Brothers (*Stranger Things*) started off with their short, *Eater*, which showed "flashes of scary genius."[2] The Russo Brothers (*Captain America: Civil War, Arrested Development*) had their career jump-started after Steven Soderbergh saw their film at a film festival.[3]

The actor, Bryce Dallas Howard, just had *Solemates*, the short film she wrote and directed, premiere at the Sundance Film Festival. We met her years ago when she took one of our writing classes. We were shocked. We asked her what she was doing there. She explained she wanted to learn more about writing. We were impressed.

THE BOOK WE WISH WE HAD

The book is called *Proof of Concept: Writing the Short Film* because we believe a well-written short script proves to the writer that they can write something longer that is just as good, but that short film can also get a career started, and sometimes that short film becomes a feature film. This book is designed for the "dreamer and the doer." We were once in the same seat you are now—studying. Studying screenwriting at a college or university level. We got a lot out of film school. We met our classmates who would become our future managers, and future development people. We learned a lot from each other. The opportunities of using New York City as a backlot was something we would never trade and we believe everyone should live in the capital of the world at least once. However, when it came to learning how to write a screenplay, we learned nothing. Zero. Zip. And we learned nothing about how to write a short film, which was the thesis part of the program.

A group of us recognized this and "self-educated." We would read scripts, talk about movies and groundbreaking television. And we would write. It didn't matter if it was good, it mattered that we were getting better. Right after graduating film school, our education began. We jumped in the waters and learned to swim with the sharks. Juliet worked as a reader (a script analyst) for Robert DeNiro and Tribeca Productions. Keith worked as a writer's assistant for Andy Breckman (*Monk, Rat Race*) one of the hottest writers in Hollywood who didn't want to be in Hollywood. He never left New Jersey. By working in the real world, we learned the right way to write a screenplay.

And we did. We worked continuously in Los Angeles for close to twenty years. Throughout our careers whenever we had an opportunity to speak in front of a class or a seminar, we found we thoroughly enjoyed passing on the practical knowledge of what we had learned. We hope this book helps.

Each chapter has multiple writing exercises. You can do them as you go along, or do them all at the end. Each writer works differently. We suggest you develop your skills and do the exercises at the conclusion of each chapter.

DEMYSTIFY THE WRITING

Our goal is to help you learn how to create moving content for any form of filmed entertainment. Why? We want to be entertained. We want to hear new voices and new stories that are reflective. We like to stay current and try to see and watch everything. Those were our working habits when we were in our twenties and they remain our working habits now that we are not in our twenties.

Aspiring writers need to write, read, and watch.

If you're not writing, you have nothing to show people; nothing to direct; nothing to re-write. You have an idea that might stay parked in your brain forever and never get on the page.

If you're not reading (scripts and book) then you are not studying your craft. Classic screenplays can be found online. Sites like simplyscripts.com or dailyscript.com are terrific resources.

If you're not watching movies and television, you are not being "influenced" by the medium. The screenwriter Shane Black says: "I've read a thousand private-eye novels." He's name-checked Raymond Chandler as an influence.[4] If you are not watching, you are also not learning how an audience reacts. You need to go to a movie theater and see movies with an audience. You need to see the hot new show. You need to be in the seat.

And you should listen . . .

When we were in film school, guest speakers would come to campus about once a month to talk about their career and show their latest work. Now, you have thousands of writers sharing their stories about their process on many, many, great podcasts. You should be listening to:

- ► Filmspotting
- ► On Story
- ► On the Page
- ► ScriptNotes
- ► The Q&A with Jeff Goldsmith
- ► The Treatment
- ► The Writers Panel/Nerdist

Opening Credits

In our opening credits we'd like to thank everyone whoever let us in a classroom. That's the Television, Radio & Film Department at S.I. Newhouse School of Public Communications at Syracuse University, and the English & Creative Writing Department at SUNY Oswego.

We also want to thank Brandon Borke and Brenda Rolwes at Kendall Hunt Publishing. And Joel Kaplan—he knows why. And to Elena DeLuccia, our assistant on this project for all her hard work.

We especially want to thank our daughters, Sabrina and Ava. Both are named after Billy Wilder movies (*Sabrina* and *Avanti*). They grew up with parents who are screenwriters and somehow survived. They love stories and we love telling them stories. Their brilliance and kindness never ceases to amaze us. They are and will forever be our two best credits.

ENDNOTES

1. http://www.indiewire.com/2016/08/duplass-brothers-short-film-this-is-john-watch-sundance-1201714331/

2. http://www.indiewire.com/2016/08/duffer-brothers-short-film-eater-stranger-things-directors-1201713815/

3. https://en.wikipedia.org/wiki/Russo_brothers

4. http://grantland.com/features/the-twisted-career-hollywood-bad-boy-shane-black/

CHAPTER 1

What Is a Screenplay?

Many years ago when David Letterman was hosting *Late Night*, he went around New York City asking random people on the street, "What's your screenplay about?"

It seemed like everyone in New York City was working on a screenplay.

What Is a Screenplay Anyway?

> A screenplay has many definitions. Wikipedia describes a screenplay as: *a written work by screenwriters for a film, video game, or television program. These screenplays can be original works or adaptations from existing pieces of writing. In them, the movement, actions, expression, and dialogues of the characters are also narrated. A play for television is also known as a teleplay.*[1]

As usual with Wiki, the definition says a lot and not much at all. You are writing something that, when it gets filmed, has the potential to be seen by millions of people in the world. It's more than just dialogue and actions: It's a *story*. There's so much written about writing a screenplay, and lucky for you we've read most of it. For us, there is a clear definition of a screenplay that every professional should know.

A SCREENPLAY IS A MOVIE IN WRITTEN FORM

Technically, it is also a document that informs all members of the production crew how to budget, cast, design, costume, and shoot the movie. But before all that, someone has to want to make the movie. So the writer of a screenplay should always begin with the end result in mind. You want the reader of the screenplay to walk away as if they have just seen a movie. Reading a screenplay should elicit the same emotional response one would get from seeing the finished product in a theater.

And that is the sign of a great screenplay. Studio executives read hundreds of screenplays a year, and script analysts read even more. They all yearn for the ones they can't put down because they want to know what happens next. If they finish the screenplay and have seen the movie clearly in their mind, chances are it's a very well-written story.

Professional writers follow this mantra: Put the movie on the page. Dan Gilroy's *Nightcrawler* does away with any technical descriptions of INT (Interior) and EXT (Exterior). He learned this from his brother Tony (*The Bourne Identity, Michael Clayton*), and they learned from their New York neighbor William Goldman, who is the godfather of the modern-day screenwriter. Our advice: read and watch everything from Goldman, who created the spec-screenplay marketplace with his sale of *Butch Cassidy and the Sundance Kid*. You might know him as the writer of the novel and screenplay for *The Princess Bride*.

Please take a moment and think about the word "screen." How has it evolved in the last one hundred years? We now watch scripted entertainment in movie theaters, on television, computer screens, and our phones. It's not possible to film a blank page. Therefore, every one of these platforms needs some form of a script. Now, we are sure someone is asking, "What about 'reality' television shows?" Dirty secret: someone is actually writing those too. Reality television refuses to acknowledge this for their brand identity and to keep the writers from being paid fairly. Reality TV doesn't provide writers with health and benefits or a pension. The reality of reality TV is that they are not fair to writers. So we will never speak of reality TV again.

What about shows like *Curb Your Enthusiasm* that rely on improv (improvisation)? Well, even though the show draws heavily on spontaneity, the actors work from an outline that was written by creator Larry David, who is in almost every scene of each episode. He also won an Emmy for writing a show called *Seinfeld*, and prior to that, wrote many movies and plays. He is a *writer*.

In the early 2010s, a form of this improv method migrated and appeared in independent feature films like the Duplass Brothers' *The Puffy Chair*, Lynn Shelton's *HumpDay*, and Joe Swanberg's *Drinking Buddies* and *Happy Christmas*. This style is the American form of "Mumblecore"—movies that are very low budget and feature improvised dialogue. We think both *Drinking Buddies* and *Happy Christmas* missed the mark because they weren't scripted at all. For the movie *The One I Love*, screenwriter Justin Lader followed the *Curb Your Enthusiasm* approach and production began with a fifty-five page outline or "scriptment" for the movie. As they neared production, it became clear to him he needed to write the last thirty pages. He talked about this with scriptshadow.net, saying, "As pre-production rolled along it became apparent that the last 30 minutes of the movie required full scripting for practical reasons that would have made improv difficult."[2]

On television, *Louie* and *Broad City* have a similar improv feel. But before anything goes to camera, someone is writing the script. As one of *Broad City*'s stars and creators, Ilana Glazer, said to *Business Insider*: "Writing is the first act of our three act experience of the show of acting, shooting, editing."[3]

Scripts are written by the *screenwriter*. Screenwriters are, and will always be, the first person to "see" the movie when they write it down.

Genres

Movies and television are written and categorized in **genres.** That is, what kind of movie is it? How do you describe it? In *The Atlantic*'s must-read article by Alexis C. Madrigal entitled "How Netflix Reverse Engineered Hollywood," Madrigal highlights that "through a combination of elbow grease and spam-level repetition, we discovered that Netflix possesses not several hundred genres, or even several thousand, but 76,897 unique ways to describe types of movies."[4]

76,897! Wow. We never realized "Violent Thrillers About Cats" was a genre. Or "Chilling Goofy Movies." Or that "Romantic Comedy Crime" movies were a thing.

It's great for their algorithm, but it's never going to work with a studio executive. The rule is to keep it simple. Why is it important for a screenwriter to "know their genre"? When you're writing, you want to keep your tone consistent. Certain genres consistently have "different" tropes that a writer can play with. Comedies tend to end happily. Dramas—not so much. So when we talk about **genres**, here is our list. And they happen to be the only ones we've heard in a producer or studio executive's office. Then again, we have yet to pitch to Netflix.

We love to stay current. We know the history of movies from its inception to well, *Inception*, to reading the scripts of movies and shows that are coming out next year. We know the entertainment business is always changing and while it's very important to know the classics, it is equally important to go to the movies and sit in an audience. *Feel* how the audience reacts to the trailers and to the movie itself. We will be using current references throughout this book and **we suggest you watch the movies and read the screenplays we cite in this book.**

ROMANTIC COMEDY is also known as the "Romcom." They tend to be funny and light-hearted with the stakes centering around a romance between two main characters. They tend to end happily with couples uniting. Examples: *Trainwreck, Forgetting Sarah Marshall, 500 Days of Summer.*

BROAD COMEDY refers to comedies that don't rely on romance to push the story forward. They tend to have more physical comedy than verbal banter, and are often less grounded in reality. These physical comedy scenes are typically called "set pieces," or rather, a sustained series of physical hijinks. Think about Fat Amy in *Pitch Perfect 2* or the horse in *Daddy's Home,* the party in *Sisters,* and everything in *Bridesmaids.* Broad comedies might have more R-rated humor, nudity, and drug use—skewing toward a younger audience. For more examples of this, check out *The Hangover, Neighbors,* and *Spy.* Wait! We can see your hand raised in the back there. *Spy* had that romance with Susan Cooper (Melissa McCarthy) and Rick Ford (Jason Statham) and *Trainwreck* is very broad and physical. Yes, but if you take out the romance in *Spy,* the movie still works. The character of Susan Cooper still changes even if she doesn't end up with Rick.

HORROR movies are obviously meant to scare you. Directors love to stage a scene where the audience jumps out of their seats—typically known as a Jump Scene. Again, the director can't stage it unless the writer writes it. They deal with our darkest fears: things like demonic killers, supernatural entities, and haunted houses. At the center of horror films is something evil the audience fears. Recent examples you should see: *It Follows, 28 Weeks Later, The Cabin in the Woods, Let the Right One In* (see the Swedish version first).

DRAMA is the genre of real-life struggles within the human condition. They are serious, though not without levity. The subject material can range from alcoholism or drug addiction (*Trainspotting*) to racial prejudice (*12 Years a Slave*) to sports dramas (*Creed*). Dramas often end with a sense of loss. We see the emotional journey of the main characters, and although some things were gained in the struggle, there can be a feeling of despair, yet an added sense of hopefulness. That is, the characters went through hell and now things are getting better. Recent examples of this include: *Birdman (or the Unexpected Virtue of Ignorance), Room, Straight Outta Compton,* and *The Social Network*.

ROMANCE is a sub-genre of drama. Anybody who's ever been in a romantic relationship knows that romance *is* drama. These movies center around the drama that is falling in and out of love. They might deal with different situations involving courtships or unrequited love, love triangles, and infidelity. However, there's not always a "happily ever after" in love stories. There is often tragedy awaiting one or more of the main characters. Romance dramas are often meant to have members of the audience sobbing into their popcorn-stained napkins as the credits roll. Recent examples of gut-wrenching films: *The Fault in Our Stars, Blue is the Warmest Color, Y Tu Mamá También,* and *Me and Earl and the Dying Girl*.

ADVENTURE or **ACTION** is one of the more popular genres. It has enjoyed a resurgence because of the expansion of the global audience. CGI (Computer Generated Imagery) allows for tons of explosions and death-defying stunts that should only be seen on the big screen. Why are these movies so popular? The old saying is, you tell a joke to ten people and maybe five will laugh. You pull out a gun, and ten people are jumping under the table. At its core, the adventure/action movies tend to have a hero fighting to save their life, or the world, against impossible odds. Recent examples include: *The Fast and the Furious* series, *Spectre, Mission Impossible: Rogue Nation, Kingsman: The Secret Service,* and *Mad Max: Fury Road*.

THRILLER movies are intended to get your heart racing, your adrenaline pumping, and make you sit on the edge of your seat. They are filled with suspense and they often have some element of crime or espionage. There might be double-crosses and characters that are not what they appear to be. (*The Usual Suspects* anyone?) Some recent examples include: *Gone Girl, The Equalizer, Nightcrawler, The Girl with the Dragon Tattoo* (see the Swedish version over the American David Fincher version).

WAR movies are exactly that: the dramatic action of the story centers around some aspect of the horror and sacrifice that is war. They might be complete works of fiction (such as *Fury*) or based on and/or inspired by actual events such as *American Sniper, The Hurt Locker,* and *Zero Dark Thirty.*

WESTERN movies are set against the backdrop of the American West. They might involve frontiersman, cowboys, or outlaws and center around a theme of morality. They were once enormously popular, and although they have found their way back to the big screen, they have become more escapist. Recent examples include: *The Revenant, True Grit, Django Unchained,* and *Hateful Eight.*

SCIENCE FICTION (or "Sci-Fi") movies and television programs are one of the more popular genres. They center around stories that are literally out of this world (*Interstellar*) or show the possibilities or fears with advances in technology (*Ex-Machina*). They can be very cerebral (*Moon*), based on hard science (*The Martian*), or they can be an adventure with light-sabers and Han Solo, like in *Star Wars: The Force Awakens.* Other recent sci-fi movies that have hit it big with audiences are *Jurassic World, Godzilla,* and *The Hunger Games* series.

FANTASY is another genre that has soared back into relevancy since the recent CGI boom began with Peter Jackson's *The Lord of the Rings.* Fantasy revolves around mystical lands of long-ago places that may or may not be of this Earth. The adage goes like this: if there is a spaceship in it, it's science fiction. If there is a dragon, it's fantasy. (*Game of Thrones* anyone?) The fantasy genre is brimming with mythology (like the *Percy Jackson and the Olympians* series), magic (the *Harry Potter* series), and supernatural wizards whether it be Gandalf (*The Lord of the Rings* series) or a fairy godmother (*Cinderella*). One warning about this genre: much like the superhero genre to be discussed below, Hollywood has a huge appetite for fantasy stories that are based on *pre-existing* material such as novels and young adult novels. Some fantasy movies you should see are *Pan's Labyrinth, Stardust, Troll Hunter* (Norway), and *Enchanted.*

MUSICAL is a genre that has a rich history in movies. Filled with song and dance, they are usually based on a hit Broadway show much like *Hairspray, Grease, Chicago,* and *Mamma Mia.* However, the original musical has found its way into the film world. You have to thank Australian filmmaker Baz Luhrman for this when he brought *Strictly Ballroom* to movie screens. Recent original musicals are *Once* and *Moulin Rouge!* On the horizon is *La La Land,* which was written and directed by Damien Chazelle, who also wrote and directed the music-centric *Whiplash.*

ANIMATION is a genre that often combines musical elements with comedy. Some of the best films in the musical genre of the last twenty years have been Disney-animated movies like *Beauty and the Beast, The Lion King,* and *The Little Mermaid.* While *The Incredibles, Finding Nemo,* and the *Toy Story* series have no musical moments, they're still spectacular. Animation, like fantasy, is rich in mythology.

One rule for writing animation is that you should always have a reason to animate: you want to show us something we have not seen before. Remember this: animation ideas are generated *in-house*. Pixar comes up with their ideas internally, then spends years developing that idea, and finally either brings in a writer, or uses writers in-house to compose the script. It is a tough market to crack, but one that has no creative glass ceiling. Anything goes. Movies to see: *Frozen*, *Inside Out*, *Minions*, and *The Lego Movie*.

THE SUPERHERO MOVIE is now a genre. Steven Spielberg recently compared "Superhero Movies" to the western genre by predicting that they will cycle themselves out.[5] They're already hard to categorize. *The Dark Knight* is one of the best thrillers made in the last twenty years, *Iron Man* was a terrific adventure film, and *The Guardians of the Galaxy* was a joyride to the stars with a foul-mouthed raccoon and Groot so it must be science fiction like *Man of Steel*, right? So what does that make *Batman v Superman: Dawn of Justice*? In this sense, Spielberg is right, and he usually is: A movie based on an existing superhero comic should be categorized as a superhero movie.

WHAT DOES EVERY GOOD STORY DO WELL?

So what do these movies and television shows in all these different genres have in common? What does every story do to best tell a story? What does every story have in its DNA since the dawn of time and the advent of storytellers? You might say characters, dialogue, settings, and conflict—and you're right. We'll get to that soon, but first, they have something that the audience never sees: **structure**.

Stories all have a beginning, middle, and end, which can be called Acts One, Two, and Three. Furthermore, these can also be categorized as the **set-up, confrontation,** and **resolution**. First, you meet the main characters of the story, then they go on a journey of some kind where they're confronted with various obstacles, and finally their journey ends with a resolution. In long-form television series, the set-up might be the pilot, or the first episode, after which the confrontation will continue for multiple seasons. Then, if the show is lucky enough not to get cancelled, there could be some resolution for the characters in the final episode. Short films have the same tenets: beginning/set-up, middle/confrontation, and end/resolution. In the short film, *Plot Device*, the set-up is the aspiring filmmaker sitting at home looking for inspiration on the Internet as he listens to the words of a famous director. After he orders the plot device, it arrives and he is suddenly thrust into different genres (confrontation). This involves battling zombies and spaceships, experiences the subtly of indie film, and finally returns home (resolution). Or so he thinks—make sure you watch past the credits.

However, you can't keep the audience engaged with only your structure. Think of it like architecture; every building has a foundation, doors, windows, and bearing partitions. But you don't want to walk into every building—there has to be a reason to go inside.

The screenwriter gives the audience a reason to watch the story by involving them in the story. They do this by posing **questions.** If your story has the audience wondering what's going to happen next, chances are that people will keep watching, or keep swiping the script pages on their reader.

Questions are the basis of every good story. From short film to feature, or an indie breakout film to a Hollywood global blockbuster:

In *Room*, will captive mother Joy and son Jake be able to escape the room?

In *The Martian*, will smart-talking astronaut Mark Watney be able to survive alone on Mars?

In *Creed*, will Adonis, a young broker-turned-boxer, learn to be a professional fighter and come to terms with who he really is?

In *Brooklyn*, will the innocent immigrant Eilis find happiness in Brooklyn with Tony or go back to Ireland?

In *Star Wars: The Force Awakens*, will orphan desert rat Rey and ex-storm trooper Finn be able to stop Kylo Ren, defeat the First Order, and destroy the Star Killer base?

Think about all the other questions that are raised in *The Force Awakens*: Where's Luke? Who is Rey? Is she a Skywalker? A Kenobi? What is the connection with Rey and Kylo Ren? And Luke? What is Finn's backstory? How did Maz get the original lightsaber? Audiences are already waiting for the answers that will be revealed on December 15, 2017. By the way, all of these questions are subplots to the main question that is the main story line.

Go back to the previous questions for a moment: Did you notice how we phrased them? We always led with the main characters—"captive mother Joy," "Smart-talking astronaut Mark Watney," "Innocent immigrant Eilis." All stories are about SOMEONE, regardless of if they are novels, plays, TV shows, or feature films.

At the end of the setup the main question is asked, and at the end of the resolution, it has been answered.

Stories tend to be about this:

SOMEONE WANTS SOMETHING AND IS HAVING TROUBLE GETTING IT

The "someone" is your main character, the "something" is the want, the goal, and the "having trouble getting something" is the conflict.

THE SCREENWRITER AND THE AUDIENCE

We have all been to a movie where the audience bursts into applause at the end. We have also watched a great television show and couldn't wait to tell our friends about what we saw. Basically, we have all been the audience; you know what you like, and you know what moves you emotionally. A screenwriter is not writing the screenplay for themselves. Every screenplay ever written was written for an audience. It was also written to be filmed: to be seen and heard. We always tell students that they are not writing haikus (they don't pay well), but rather that they are writing something that has a chance to connect with a *global* audience. The writer might want to get their movie made, be it long-form or short, but **what does the audience want?**

Audiences want to be involved in the story—they want to go on a journey. This can be an emotional journey or a physical journey. *The Guardians of the Galaxy* begins on Earth and goes all over the galaxy, *Room* takes place in a tiny room. Each story has a journey.

Audiences also want an emotional experience. When students pitch their ideas in class we often ask, "How do you want us to feel at the end of the film? Should we be laughing? Crying? Should we feel bad?" It's ultimately your call, but you, the screenwriter, have to deliver the emotions.

Audiences want to see themselves on the screen. They want to connect with the main characters. This connection might come from a physical connection, like Rey from *Star Wars: The Force Awakens*. She is a strong-willed protagonist and young women love her. Heck, everyone loves her, she's Rey. We love the diversity that makes up the characters of *Star Wars: The Force Awakens*. But just because a character looks like a member of the audience doesn't mean there will be a connection. In the TV series, *Breaking Bad,* Walter White is a man who sells blue meth and builds a drug empire, maybe killing some people along the way. Why did an audience connect with Walter White? The answer: primal emotions.

If you take away all the meth-dealing, *Breaking Bad* is really about a dying man who loves his family and wants to provide for them after his death—so he's willing to do anything in order for this to happen. That love is **a primal emotion**.

Love, hate, revenge, and survival are all examples of primal emotions. See if you can think of a few more. If your story can be reduced to a primal emotion that the audience has experienced before, you connect with the audience.

In *The Pursuit of Happyness,* Will Smith stars as Chris Gardner in the true story of his nearly one-year ordeal of being homeless as he struggles to care for his son (love, family), find a job, a place to live. They need to survive. In *Jurassic World*, Owen and Claire want to stay alive and save Claire's niece and nephew. The same primal emotion exists in both of these films. We have never been to Mars, but in *The Martian* we want to see if Mark Watney will survive. Freedom is one of the primal emotions in *12 Years a Slave* and *Mad Max: Fury Road*. Both Solomon Northup and Imperator Furiosa want the same thing. These are two completely different movies, yet similar in this aspect.

Audiences also like to see **shared experiences**—experiences that all of us go through in life and have to deal with. The movie *Neighbors* is a great example. From the title alone we know what the movie is going to be about and can guess where the conflict originates. It's from the shared experience of having lousy neighbors who play their music too loudly and don't invite us to their great parties. Think about the movie *Inside Out* which personifies joy, sadness, fear, anger, and disgust; at some point, we have all imagined that there are people in our head helping us make everyday decisions. Okay, maybe not, but we do recognize that we are often ruled by our emotions. A shared experience might also be a phrase or an expression that is in the zeitgeist. *Unfriended* was a low-budget but effective horror movie that played off the social media expression used on Facebook. *Horrible Bosses* tapped into the shared experience of having a horrible boss. *The Hangover*? You get it.

Audiences also connect with **common elements** in stories. The *Harry Potter* series took place in a magical castle with wizards and magic wands. We have nothing in common with that, and we don't know any school kid who does. So what was the connection with the audience? Each new *Harry Potter* story dealt with school, making new friends, making new enemies, and having professors you don't like very much. That is something that most audiences have in common with the magical character of Harry Potter. The common element of the highly-successful *Fast and Furious* movies is summed up in one line from the movie: "I don't have friends, I got family." Those crazy racers are a "family" and that's why audiences love their death-defying, reality-bending escapades. What about *Straight Outta Compton*? It's a story about achieving your dreams despite your circumstances of being unable to create art and music.

A Blueprint for Production

Often, a screenwriter will write many drafts and rewrites of a screenplay as it goes toward production. The first draft will be to see if the film studio likes the script enough to make the movie, the second draft will be rewritten to entice actors to come on board, and the final drafts will focus on the technical aspects included in the screenplay to inform the filmmakers how the movie is actually going to be produced.

As we said, a screenplay is first and foremost a movie in written form, however, it is also a blueprint with precise formatting specific for production. Filmmaking professionals can quickly glance at a screenplay without reading it and see if it's a professionally written script worth their time.

ENDNOTES

1. https://en.wikipedia.org/wiki/Screenplay

2. http://scriptshadow.net/screenwriter-interview-justin-lader-the-one-i-love/

3. http://www.businessinsider.com/broad-city-tv-show-writing-process-2015-3

4. http://www.theatlantic.com/technology/archive/2014/01/how-netflix-reverse-engineered-hollywood/282679/

5. http://www.hollywoodreporter.com/heat-vision/steven-spielberg-predicts-superhero-movies-819768

CHAPTER 2

Visual Storytelling

THEY'RE CALLED MOTION PICTURES

Imagine this opening scene: A father stands in his backyard. He throws a Frisbee to his daughter. As the Frisbee sails into the air, he remembers the day she was born and how she grew up; how he held her in his arms after she fell when learning to walk; how he stayed up all night when she was in the hospital. He remembers every key moment in her life. If this was a novel, it might be seven pages before the daughter catches the Frisbee.

We're not writing novels. We are not conveying long interior, stream-of-consciousness monologues. We are writing a movie. The same scene in the movie would be: "The father throws the Frisbee to his daughter. She catches it."

In this chapter, we will focus on all the writing that occurs in the action blocks of a screenplay—or rather, all the text that is not dialogue. Most screenwriting software programs refer to this writing as "action." Movies are pictures with words (i.e., dialogue) and we think it's better to learn to write without the words (dialogue).

MOVIES are written to be SEEN.

NOVELS are written to be READ.

But, the new writer insists: I need the dialogue to tell the audience what is happening. No, you don't need dialogue, you need Eisenstein. Huh? Is he in the class?

Sergei Mikhailovich Eisenstein was a <u>Soviet film director</u> and <u>film theorist</u>, a pioneer in the theory and practice of montage starting his career in the 1920s.[1] Montage is the foundation of visual storytelling. The cutting away to different shots creates different emotions. Here is one example that has been used for many years.

1. Show a close-up of an actor looking blankly at the camera.
2. Show their point-of-view (what they are looking at). Let's say it's a bowl of soup.
3. Cut back to shot #1.

When asked what they saw on the screen, audiences would say, a man who is hungry. Here is what Eisenstein did with montage. He changes the middle shot, which changes the emotion. So . . .

1. Show a close-up of an actor looking blankly at the camera.
2. Show a coffin.
3. Cut back to shot #1.

The audience now would say they saw a man in mourning. It's the same close-up that was used earlier. The actor did not change his expression. He did not act. The contrast of the images and the sequence of the images created the emotions.

One more time . . .

1. Show a close-up of an actor looking blankly at the camera.
2. Show a beautiful woman.
3. Cut back to shot #1.

Audiences will say that they are watching a man in love. Again, it's the same close-up for all three "montages." The only thing that changes is the shot in-between the two close-ups which changes the emotion. By the way, we always talk about influences. One of the greatest sequences ever directed is the famous "Odessa Steps" sequence in *Battleship Potemkin* (1925). Find it on the Internet. Then look for "The Untouchables—Union State Scene" on YouTube. The director, Brian DePalma (due to budget restraints), created a masterful homage to Eisenstein. *The Untouchables'* Union Station scene remains the most obvious allusion to the Odessa Steps sequence.[2]

The scene was written before being filmed.

You might be saying: Eisenstein was almost 100 years ago. We argue that once a hit, always a hit. Pixar has used visual montage to make people laugh and cry and to emotionally connect.

Wall-E is close to being a silent movie. Wall-E's life on Earth contained sadness, humor, loneliness, hope, and little to no dialogue. Wall-E's love for Eve was all about the juxtaposition of the shots. Their "hand-holding" and dance among the stars was total romance.

The opening sequence of *Up* is a scene that all writers should study and deconstruct. Director Pete Docter says of the opening, "From a 'feel' standpoint, it was the sense of a life lived, and not only the highs, but the lows. That's why we put in a couple of dark moments, like their not being able to have children, and of course, her passing away, so the scene didn't feel like a total Pollyanna thing. It actually feels more real, and I think that's how you remember life being like."[3]

We see that life lived as Carl and Elie meet and fall in love. We see transitions visually provide information as they look at clouds and see babies; to the painting of a baby's room, to crying in a doctor's office as they learn they can't have children.

We SEE Carl and Elie saving money to see the world but blown tires, house repairs, and broken limbs get in the way. Later when they're old and they clean the house, the money jar is in the background on the shelf symbolizing discarded dreams.

We SEE them go from young to old as in the beginning of the montage they rush up a hill; as they get older they trudge up the hill until Elie falls on the hill.

We SEE their life.

But you might argue that you're not writing *Up,* that you're writing a short film. Writing a short film is the same as writing a feature. Visual information is always better.

For a short film, one of the best examples of visual storytelling is a film called *Floating,* directed by Greg Jardin. The logline is: "Fragile and lonely, a being made up of balloons wanders L.A. looking for connection."[4] The entire movie is dialogue free and conveys themes of loneliness and togetherness with the same emotional force as Pixar's *Up.*

Introducing Characters through Visuals

Characters are usually introduced visually through action. One of the opening sequences of *Schindler's List* introduces us to Oscar Schindler as he tries to impress the Nazi regime. As the music plays and very little dialogue is spoken we SEE Schindler as a successful businessman, tipping waiters, impressing the Nazis as he never moves from his chair.

The first shot of John Ford's iconic *The Searchers* has a door opening. We see a woman in silhouette watching the approach of Ethan Edwards (John Wayne), the Civil War vet. The last shot is the mirror, framed in the doorway. Ethan, having fulfilled his mission, walks away. If you have ever played the video game *Fallout* you might think these images are familiar.

In the short film, *Gridlock,* we meet the main character stuck in his car in traffic and popping pills. From that shot, we know this is a short-tempered man.

The short film, *God of Love,* opens with a voice-over, but when we first SEE Ray he is a singer, a romantic who is very good at darts.

In Shawn Christensen's short film, *Curfew,* we see the protagonist, Richie, lying in his bathtub, bleeding out from a suicide attempt when the phone rings.

VISUALIZE THE EXPOSITION AND THEME

Exposition is best when visualized. So how do we visualize exposition? You don't want to do the "film school" thing and have a character hold up a note like a story card in a silent movie. You want the characters to SEE things that are important to them and to the plot.

You also want the audience to watch the story unfold and to figure things out. We mentioned the coin jar in *Up* as visual exposition to see the passage of time and to provide information. This is a great use of an object to provide exposition to an audience.

In Alfred Hitchcock's *Notorious,* our heroes, played by Cary Grant and Ingrid Bergman, have to sneak into the wine cellar and obtain information. They have to do this before the champagne runs out. As the sequence starts we see many bottles of champagne on ice. The sequence plays out with repeated cuts back to the champagne bottles on ice. Each time there are fewer and fewer bottles indicating time is running out.

Images also convey exposition. The images could be a woman crying as she finds a red bra in her husband's briefcase, a student rolling up a shirt to reveal test answers written on their arm, and a man hiding a half-eaten Snickers bar under a pillow. All of these images let us know that someone is cheating, and since they're hidden, it indicates that it's bad.

The big reveal in *Breaking Bad* is when Hank finally realized his brother-in-law, Walter White, is the Heisenberg—the meth king he has been hunting. His only clue is the initials W.W. which he joked in an earlier episode could be Willy Wonka or even Walter White. So how is this exposition revealed? How does Hank find the evidence he needs to realize Walt is the bad guy? As Hank sits in a bathroom, he grabs a book that has been sitting there for a while. Inside is a dedication to: W.W.

We are not trying to be crude, but it was genius on the part of the *Breaking Bad* team to have the biggest "oh shit" moment take place in a bathroom as Hank sits on a toilet.

Visualize the Theme

The garbage bag floating in *American Beauty*, and the Maltese falcon in the movie of the same name visualize the theme of the story. When asked what the Maltese falcon is, Sam Spades answers: "the stuff dreams are made of." The Maltese falcon turns out to be worthless.

One of the best examples of a short film visualizing the theme is the short film *The Apocalypse*. The idea and theme is, if you had a thought in your head, your head would explode. And that is what happens. We see heads exploding. It happens to anchors on the news. It happens to a dog who thinks about chasing a ball. And the only people left standing are two people who do not have a thought in their heads.

In *Inja Dog,* a short film about the violence and inhumanity of Apartheid in South Africa, the "character arc" of the dog carries the theme of how hatred and racism only brings death.

In the short film *Oppressed Majority*, the world is turned on its head. Men are the stay-at-home dads and housekeepers. Women are the breadwinners. Women are the ones who whistle and harass men as they walk around town. The entire film is an effective commentary on sexism.

WRITING THE VISUALS

When we read a screenplay, we're visualizing what is happening on the screen at the very moment it occurs. The screenwriter can typically only write what the audience is seeing. Because we see it as it happens, <u>we always write in the present tense</u>. This means you can't write about something that the hero saw *yesterday*. When we're watching a character riding his bike to school, there's no way to know that he broke up with his girlfriend the day before. If you want the audience to know that, you'd need to show them that scene. You could show this in a previous scene before our hero rides his bike. Or, you could write it into a FLASHBACK. But even then, you'd be writing the scene in the present tense. Why? Because we're watching the scene unfold. So even though it happened in the past, it's not the past for the audience. Additionally, you can't write what the character is thinking or worrying about—at least not in the action block. A character's innermost thoughts can only come out through dialogue, even if that means that a character is talking to themselves. Or you could use a VOICE-OVER (V.O.). We'll talk about that in the chapter on dialogue.

When writing action blocks, you always need to re-read your sentences and ask yourself: HOW DO WE KNOW? We often use the acronym HDWK as a shorthand, and if you're writing something that's not clear from looking at the script, it's a HDWK moment. Consider a better way to get that information across. If the action block reads: *Nick and Tina rush into a hotel room. They just got married.* How could we know they just got married? Try this: *Nick and Tina burst into a hotel room. Nick rips off Tina's wedding dress.* By using the specific noun, "wedding dress," we know that they just got married.

Let's consider another example: *Donna drives home. She just got fired.* Now if all we can see is a woman driving her car, there's no way to know that she's driving home. There's also no way to know that she just got fired—that's a HDWK moment. Unless we hear her talking about driving home or see her pull into a driveway in front of a house, we probably can't know that she's driving home. And even then, we won't know if it's really her house from looking at the visuals. But we can easily show that she got fired. Here's how:

> Donna drives. Teary-eyed. She glances at a pink slip next to her. We see the words, "TERMINATION." She crumples the paper. Tosses it into a box crammed with plants, photographs, office supplies, and files.

Now it's clear that she was fired and it's no longer a HDWK moment.

Learning how to write visually can be tricky at first. Your goal is to take what's in your head and put it on the page so the audience can envision your story. You already know that you need to write in the present tense, and you also need to decide what details to include and what to leave out. The danger is writing too much, so don't include every little detail. For example, if you have a scene where a character walks out of her house and gets into her car, it's <u>not</u> necessary to write the following:

> Samantha walks out of the front door and closes it. She walks down three steps. She unlocks her car and opens the door. She climbs in. She takes her keys out of her purse. She turns on the engine. She checks her mirror and puts on her seatbelt. She backs out of the driveway slowly. She pulls away and drives off.

Instead you would write:

> Samantha walks out of the house and gets into her car. She drives away.

Yes, it's true that the actress playing Samantha might unlock the car, and we'd hope she would put on her seat belt and check her mirrors, but let's leave that for the actress to decide. If we include everything, we'll not only bore our reader, but our story will also run too long and we'll go over that page count. Screenwriting is like swimming in a lap pool. You have to tell your story in a pre-scribed number of pages.

Everything Is Action

In addition to writing in the present tense, we also want to use action verbs when writing a screen-play, because "the power of the action verb lies in the meaning and intention that they contain and how they bring direction and force to the sentence."[5]

Let's consider one of the most overused verbs in screenplays and turn it into an action verb. The verb, "walk," used simply, means to get from point A to B using your legs. But when we watch a movie, characters walk in a variety of ways. And how they walk can give us insight to their char-acter and what's happening in the scene—this is what we need to get across when writing a script. Let's go to the thesaurus and discover some different words for walk:

> *amble, bounce, hike, hobble, jaunt, limp, march, mosey, parade, plod, race, run, saun-ter, shuffle, skip, sprint, stagger, step, stomp, stride, stroll, strut, swagger, tramp, tread, trek, trot, tiptoe, trudge, waddle, wander*

Now let's consider our earlier scene with Samantha getting into her car and replace the word "walk" to one of our action verbs.

> *Samantha skips out of the house.* We know Samantha is happy.
> *Samantha stomps out of the house.* It's implied that Samantha is angry.
> *Samantha sprints out of the house.* We know Samantha's late for something.

By using a more specific verb for walk, we can quickly give the audience additional information and more importantly, we save space in our screenplay because we don't have to include this addi-tional information in the writing. It makes for a more interesting story through possible visual cues.

Using action verbs also helps to avoid using the screenwriter's worst nightmare: the adverb. It's true that adverbs work for other types of writing such as novels, poetry, and nonfiction. But in screenplay writing, they take up space and keep us from getting to the point. Let's consider our favorite overused verb again and add an adverb to make things worse.

> *He walks slowly.* What's a better way to write that? *He trudges.*
> *She walks proudly.* Better if we write: *She parades.*
> *He walks quietly.* See how the sentence improves when we write: *He tiptoes.*

Basically, whenever you're tempted to use an adverb, don't. See if there's a way to use an action verb instead.

High school English teachers are famous for telling their students to increase their use of specifics in their writing. Guess what? Screenplay writing requires specifics too. For example, if a character is drinking in a scene, instead of saying, *"Bob drinks at the bar,"* say, *"Bob tosses back a second Budweiser."* That's a lot different than: *"Bob sips his wine."* Both examples give us more insight into Bob's character than the generic first example. Making your nouns more specific brings life to the story and makes for a more compelling read which makes the reader want to continue turning the pages. Your script will never get produced if the reader puts it down and stops reading. So keep those verbs active and make those nouns specific.

So who is this "reader"? The reader is the first person to read your script. They're someone who can help move your story forward and ever-closer to production—or they can stop it in its tracks, causing your script to hit the proverbial trash can. Half the challenge of screenwriting is getting someone to read your script and *finish* reading it. Some executives are famous for saying they'll give a script ten pages. If it's not good by page ten, they put the script down. So make sure those first ten pages are great and remember that your screenplay is only the first step toward the end product: a *movie.*

A good story with strong visuals and interesting characters is the best way to keep a reader's attention. However, if a good story is buried in improper formatting and pages are difficult to read, a reader could just as easily put down a script even if the story is fantastic. So, it helps if you keep the following practical tips in mind when writing the action blocks of your screenplay. Here's what we recommend to make your script an easier read:

White on the Page

This refers to the blank parts of a script page. Typically, dialogue adds a bit of visually-pleasing white on the page because the lines of dialogue are indented on both sides. But what if you're writing two pages of pure action? Consider a chase on foot or by car. There might not be any dialogue, so how do we add white to the page? You can do this by breaking up the action in a variety of ways. First and foremost, we want to make sure each action block runs no longer than three to four lines. After the fourth line, start a new paragraph. Another way to break up the action is to draw emphasis to a specific action or prop. Then start a new paragraph, but this time, put THE SPECIFIC ACTION in CAPITAL LETTERS. You can do this manually, however, most screenplay software allows you to click on the word "Direction" instead of "Action" in order to put the sentence in all capital letters. Let's consider an example here:

> We're writing a car chase scene where the cars zip around tight corners, over bridges, through markets, and then, finally, the car blows up. That's a lot of information. It's going to take longer to visualize than just the ten seconds it might time out at from looking at the page. This is a scene that would be better if we broke up the action. We could put everything on a separate line or add more detail. Here's how:

THE CARS ZIP AROUND TIGHT STREET CORNERS
The Porsche roars past the cop car. Missing a street sign.
The Porsche races onto

THE BRIDGE
The cop car gains on the Porsche. Catches up. Rides alongside.
The Porsche exits the bridge. Plows

THROUGH STREET MARKETS
Shopkeepers duck out of the way. The cop car bears down on the
Porsche. A stray dog wanders into their path. The Porsche swerves.
Avoids the dog but

CRASHES INTO A BRICK WALL
The cop car brakes in time.
We watch as

THE PORSCHE BLOWS UP

Now that gives us a lot more "white on the page." It also helps us visualize exactly what's happening and keeps our reader's attention.

Your reader needs to SEE the movie when they're reading it. And you have to SEE the movie before you can write it.

ENDNOTES

1. https://en.wikipedia.org/wiki/Sergei_Eisenstein

2. http://www.denofgeek.com/us/movies/18343/iconic-movie-scene-the-untouchables%E2%80%99-union-station-shoot-out

3. http://articles.latimes.com/2010/feb/25/entertainment/la-etw-pete-docter25-2010feb25

4. https://www.shortoftheweek.com/2014/08/13/floating/

5. grammar.yourdictionary.com/parts-of-speech/verbs/Action-Verbs.html

WRITING VISUALLY

Coming up with ideas can be difficult, and coming up with a story that has no dialogue can be even more difficult. Yet, film is visual. So we need to understand how to create visual stories. Here's a way to generate a story that can be told with only visuals. A story that might take you out of your comfort zone and force you to create something entirely new.

1. Sit down with a magazine.

2. Beginning with the cover page, thumb through every page.

3. When an image grabs your attention, tear it out.

4. By the end of the magazine, you should have at least 10 images.

5. Now look at the images and choose the three that are most compelling for you.

6. Paste the three images on the next page.

NOW TELL A STORY ABOUT THESE THREE IMAGES. GIVE THEM A CONFLICT.

What happened just before
this image was taken?

What happened just before
this image was taken?

What happened just before
this image was taken?

CHAPTER 3

Dialogue

"We are Groot."
"I am not in danger. I *am* the danger."
"I'm gonna have to science the shit out of this."
"Dating you is like dating a StairMaster!"
"I am the Captain now."

Do you recognize any of the lines above? Chances are you do. When you first heard them spoken by characters in a movie, they probably resonated with you on some emotional level. You laughed. You cried. You cheered.

When you heard the lines in the context of character and the plot—you reacted. The character on the screen said what you wish you could have said if you were in their situation. You may have repeated those lines or used them in a meme, but long before the actor spoke those lines, there's a good chance they were written by the writer. Too many movie-goers and TV-watchers still believe that the actor makes up their lines. Not true. And if it is, you probably have a bad movie on your hands and a very bad, but very powerful, actor.

As much as we might love to quote great movie lines, great lines are only a small part of crafting dialogue.

Dialogue is one of the toughest parts of screenwriting. It doesn't matter whether it's for the small screen or big screen. Dialogue has to sound real but <u>not</u> be real at the same time. It has to reveal exposition without being overly expositional. It has to be brief and clever. Good dialogue flows from emotion, event, and character.

Good dialogue is the wind in the screenplay's sails. Bad dialogue is the iceberg that sinks the ship with the screenplay onboard.

We feel emerging writers wrongly believe that dialogue is the easy part of the screenwriting process. It seems easy. It's not as technical as slug lines.

New writers believe if they can tell, they don't have to show (you know what we're talking about since you've read the Visual Writing chapter). The new screenwriter believes they can have characters that talk like themselves and everything will be fine. We read many student scripts where the dialogue is long, bloated, and filled with characters whose dialogue might as well be part of a Jenna Marbles vlog. The dialogue goes on and on with the same note.

One very important thing to remember is that DIALOGUE IS OFTEN THE LAST THING WRITTEN IN A SCREENPLAY. The professional writer knows the story, the scene, and what they want to happen in the scene before they let the characters speak. They know the intent of the scene and how it fits into the overall story line. An old screenwriter once said, "The script is almost done. All I have to do is write the dialogue."

THE PURPOSE OF DIALOGUE

Why is dialogue even needed? Film is a visual language—you can turn off the sound to a movie and you should be able to follow the plot just by watching the visuals. The same holds true for TV shows today. This was not the case years ago. Television has become more cinematic since most of the audience now has a widescreen TV in their home. *Game of Thrones* can be watched and understood without the dialogue. Even *with* the dialogue, we often get confused. But that has to do with the backstory, so the main action of the episode is easy to follow visually. Sure, you would lose backstory and political intrigue but when Tyrion kills his father, Tywin, who is sitting on the throne—no one needs to say a word. Revenge is served.

Good dialogue always tells us about the characters, while bad dialogue tells us about the writer.

Bad dialogue is forced, over-expository, and doesn't have any subtext. It's attributed to characters that might be called "Harry the Explainer": The character spews information and does nothing else. This means that the writer has not done their work; they don't know the story, and more importantly, they don't know their characters.

Good dialogue reveals character, attitude, and also provides insight. This is why it's so important for the screenwriter to know their characters before they begin writing the dialogue. A good writer will lie awake at night agonizing whether or not their character would ever say a certain line. How do they find that perfect line? Are you able to find the perfect dialogue for your character? As Jon McClane (played by Bruce Willis) affirms in *Die Hard*: "Yippee-Ki-Yay, Motherfucker."

Dialogue Is the Emotional DNA of the Character

The "Yippee-Ki-Yay" line comes out of McClane's character. Hans Gruber labels McClane a cowboy and McClane rolls with it. The axiom from Aristotle has always been that "action is character." We believe that dialogue is the emotional DNA of character. Characters react to what is happening on the screen and they reveal their emotional core via dialogue. This includes what they are feeling at that moment and their point-of-view of the world. McClane is a cowboy who is going to stop at nothing to save his wife. "Yippee-Ki-Yay" is a cowboy expression straight out of classic American westerns.

Dialogue needs to be **character-specific** and the persons speaking must have a clear point-of-view. Not only should dialogue reflect the character that is speaking, but also who the character is speaking to. Dialogue needs to be in the *character's* voice and your characters should never sound the same. They don't act the same, they don't look the same—so why should they sound the same? People are different and different is good. It balances your story and it's more reflective of society.

Let's look at a simple line that might be in any script: *Get out of here*. It's a basic line of dialogue that's very clear in its purpose, yet it is also very generic. The line reveals nothing about character and there's no indication of who might be saying that line. You have to become your characters when writing their dialogue.

If we change the line *Get out of here* to *I wish you to leave*, what does that tell us about who is saying the line? *I wish you to leave*. Who speaks like that? Maybe someone who is British, someone educated, someone of a higher status, or someone who is maybe a little timid and shies away from confrontation. The intent of the words is the same; the character is now revealed through their use of words.

What if we had changed the same line to: *Get the hell out of here*. Again, it's different now and seems to be spoken more forcefully. Probably spoken by someone angrier or more direct. But it's still kind of on the generic side. What if we changed it to: *You're leaving right now. You can walk out or be carried out. Your choice*. What does that say about the character? Controlled. Angry. Confident.

What if the line needed to be spoken by a character that was broken-hearted, but determined to stay strong? The *Get out of here* might change to *All my life I wanted you to stay, now I want you not to stay*. The dialogue reflects the emotional character and a change in character.

If your character were a successful hip-hop star at the top of her game, how would she speak to people? Would it be different than someone who is a faded glory?

Every character needs to speak in their own voice. How would Deadpool say the simple words: "I love you"? You bet there would be raunchiness involved.

You, the writer has to know who the characters are before you begin writing them. Oftentimes we work with a list of character traits. If your character is angry all the time, chances are their tone and dialogue will be this way. Their dialogue reflects that. We like to make a list of our characters with specific character traits, and then run all the dialogue through that filter.

The Motivation of Dialogue or Dialogue Is Motivated

In the movie *Whiplash*, Fletcher (played by J.K. Simmons) has a character trait that might be categorized as "mean," but his meanness comes out of his backstory of wanting to find greatness in students. He hasn't been able to do this until he sees and hears Andrew (Miles Teller). Fletcher stays true to his character and pushes Miles harder and harder. His dialogue is motivated by passion to find the best in his student.

Dialogue Sets the Mood and the Tone

Let's imagine a scenario of a family moving into a haunted house but they don't know it's haunted. This could be a horror movie like *The Conjuring* or the beginning of the Seth Rogen comedy you are writing. Knowing the mood and the tone of your movie informs every line of the dialogue. Perhaps early on we see the new homeowners in bed where they start hearing noises. They open the door and see the haunted image of an older woman who used to live in that house. In a straightforward horror movie, the homeowner would scream, which is a grounded reaction. Did they actually see what they think they saw? In the comedy, the husband might scream first. Then the wife might ask, "Did you see that dead lady?" And the "Seth Rogen" character could respond in a number of ways to carry the tone of the movie. He might say, "Yes, she looked like your mother." In one of the genres, the dialogue is played straight to the audience. The other, not so much. Either way, the dialogue and reactions set the tone.

Dialogue Needs to Exist in the Moment

Actors are often told they have to live in the moment of the scene. Nothing else matters except what is unfolding at that time. Writers and their characters have to do the same. For example, in the classic film *Raiders of the Lost Ark*, Indiana Jones' overall goal is to get the ark, keep it from Hitler, and save the world from Nazism. But in each scene he doesn't talk about this goal. Instead, he is focused on the matter at hand. For example, after Indiana sets off on his goal to obtain the ark, he first goes to Nepal to find Marion and retrieve a medallion. The dialogue in the scene is focused on their past, her father, their conflict, and their history. Indy walks in and says, "I'm looking for your father." And when Marion replies, "You're two years too late," she doesn't need to say he's died, because of the subtext of the line. Saying "He's dead," would be too on point. Now Indy's whole reason for going to Nepal has changed, and the dialogue changes based on that moment. At no point does Indy tell Marion he needs the medallion to find the ark, so they negotiate the cost of the "bronze" piece and she tells him to come back the next day. This demonstrates another turning point as well as another "in the moment" moment. Dialogue is a reaction to what is happening in the story at that moment in the story.

We believe that the simple line "I am Groot" is an example of strong dialogue. It's not Shakespeare, but it works on its own as a running gag or echo throughout the movie and each time it is played it provides comic relief. Groot says nothing else in the screenplay until near the end when it looks as if the Guardians of the Galaxy are going to perish and be destroyed in a fiery explosion. Groot grows his tree-like body and envelops the team. Rocket Raccoon looks at him and informs him that he will die if he does this and asks why. This time, Groot's answer is not "I am Groot," but instead, it changes to "We are Groot." Those three words tell the audience that the Guardians are now a family as well as a team that has bonded.

When writing a story about relationships or a detective solving a mystery, writers need to worry about the small moments. Too often, young writers put too much on the page. Screenwriting is a slow burn; each line and reaction in the scene travels to the next scene, and they slowly build the structure. Physical reactions and spoken reactions also build an emotional structure.

Dialogue is reacting to the events of the story. The events push the plot forward and the dialogue reveals how the characters feel about them. **Reaction scenes** are what make up the bulk of dialogue, where characters react to the situation and move forward. When Elizabeth and Philip of *The Americans* learn their daughter Paige has figured out they're spies and starts asking lots of questions, they react to it. They decide to tell her the truth, but before they do, there are scenes of **anticipation** as they weigh the consequences of their choice. These scenes cause the reader and audience to look forward; you're taking them on a journey. Once they tell Paige, it starts all over again as they wait for her reaction and anticipate what she might do. Meanwhile, they have to go kill some people. Their life in the suburbs is very complicated.

You never want to explain the plot if you don't have to. That is the visual information and you want the characters to experience it. Here is where the dialogue comes in. The scene construction is where the hard work is, and rather than have someone tell you what happened, it is better to experience it with them and then react.

Dialogue Speaks to the Theme

Dialogue can also speak to the theme of the screenplay. This is why it is so important to know what you're writing about and what area of life you wish to explore. We are big believers in outlining and having something to say in a story. *Skyfall* is one of the most recent and more successful James Bond movies. We believe that this is because it is one of the only Bond movies where the character changes. The dialogue demonstrates the theme of getting old—reflecting back on the Bond character arc. Throughout the film, you hear terms like "old dog," "new tricks," and "dinosaur." It was a very fresh way to prop up an old franchise. Even as Eve shaves Bond's beard with a straight razor, Bond remarks on the traditional tool. Even their flirtation sticks to the theme. Bond replies, "Well, I like to do things the old fashioned way." Eve volleys back, "Sometimes the old ways are the best."

Dialogue Looks Forward

Another function of dialogue is to advance the narrative. Dialogue sometimes needs to look forward. Take these for example: if a character says, *See you at the Club!* You can bet we are going to see a club scene. *You better not miss back-to-school night!* Guess what scene is coming up: back-to-school night. The characters in the story need to be informed of what might be happening to them next. This way, the audience is also informed, and you can insert dialogue to plant an event that will pay off. What if a parent misses a "Back-to-School Night" after being told they better not miss it? As a writer, you are always setting up expectations in stories. A lot of times, the characters fall short or something derails their plans. At the beginning of the movie *Black Swan,* the ballet director tells Nina, "Devastated and doomed, the White Swan leaps off a cliff, killing herself. But in death she finds freedom." This is the entire film in one line of dialogue.

Dialogue Looks Back

Dialogue often looks back; characters reflect upon their lives at certain times in a story. It's usually later rather than earlier. Frank Underwood in *House of Cards* hated his father. He tells us this in season three as he urinates on his father's grave.

Dialogue Creates Tension

Think of any family dinner you have ever attended. Actually, just think of the ones that ended with people screaming at each other as they sat still. This is dialogue that creates *tension*. There is no better example of a screenwriter that does this well than the great Aaron Sorkin. In the opening scene from *The Social Network,* the two main characters, Mark and Erica, argue and then break apart. During this scene we learn about Final Clubs, rowing, and Mark's genius as well as his equally dismissive attitude. This shows his defensiveness while also speaking about the theme of friendship and lack thereof. Isn't that what Facebook is all about?

VEILING EXPOSITION

Exposition is what we need to know for the story to be followed by an audience. On many broadcast television shows, the exposition is revealed in dialogue. For example: *The court case is in five minutes!* Television shows suffer from the "walk and talk and sit." How much of *Scandal* or *The Americans* have scenes of people sitting on a park bench and talking about the plot? Television doesn't have the time (or the money) to present the story cinematically each week—they save that for the big events. But there are ways to deliver exposition where it does not seem like an exposition vomit. *Game of Thrones'* exposition is often revealed through a term known as "sexposition." If you have seen *Game of Thrones,* you know what we're talking about. Members of kingdoms tend to talk about how to take over the throne as their clothes are thrown all over the royal bedroom.

Exposition through conflict is always best because exposition earned is always better than exposition given. Having characters feeling reluctant and conflicted about giving up information will generate tension and assist in veiling the delivery.

Exposition through action is another way to reveal information. Look at any film by acclaimed action directors like James Cameron or Christopher Nolan. Oftentimes their characters might be giving out loads of information, but it's served to the audience in the midst of a chase scene or another action scene. So instead of realizing an exposition, it's unfolding in front of you.

CASE STUDY: DIALOGUE IN THE WORLD MARKET

The feature film writer should know visual humor now trumps verbal humor. Television and independent films are where the wit is. The studios are now into the "Wow," or the spectacle where dialogue can be globalized easily and the visual action of the story is all that matters. Case in point: *Ghostbusters* (1984) vs. *Ghostbusters* (2016).

We were speaking with a fellow screenwriter about the reboot and realized that even though we liked the new film, we could not remember a single line. The original *Ghostbusters* (1984) premiered years ago, but screenwriters and fans do recall the following memorable lines:

► "Don't cross the streams."
► "Human sacrifice, dogs and cats living together . . . mass hysteria!"
► "We've been going about this all wrong. This Mr. Stay Puft's okay! He's a sailor, he's in New York; we get this guy laid, we won't have any trouble!"
► "We came, we saw, we kicked its ass!"

Ghostbusters (2016) was a physical and visual farce. *Ghostbusters* (1984) combined good dialogue with great visual action. And if you want to see a film with great dialogue, rent the classic *Casablanca*. Yes, it's black and white, but it remains one of the most quotable movies in history.

Do and Say

There are two ways to learn about character: by looking at what a character does and what a character says. Many times, these two qualities are completely opposites. For example, one of our favorite movies is the classic *When Harry Met Sally*. At the end of the movie, Harry rushes to a New Year's Eve party where he intends on winning Sally back. Luckily, he is armed with Nora Ephron's dialogue, and it's very specific (just like we advise you). He names everything he loves about Sally along with what drives him crazy. She responds by saying, "I hate you," as they fall into a romantic kiss. She is saying one thing and doing another—demonstrating subtext and revealing her emotional DNA.

What I Say and What I Mean

Subtext is the difference between what a character says and what they mean. Good dialogue is layered and works at both levels, just like when Sally says she hates Harry. She says it but does not mean it.

DO YOU HEAR YOUR CHARACTERS?

You need to listen to the voices of your characters. Think about what traits you have assigned them: hotheaded, sad, etc. What would their responses to certain questions be? Do they sound like all the other characters in the story? Write down the dialogue and read it aloud. Rewrite it. Make it so particular to your character that there is no one else in the story that can say the same line. Give them a clear POINT-OF-VIEW on their situation. What is their attitude toward the world? In Kevin Williamson's recent TV reboot of the Nicolas Meyer film *Time After Time*, H.G. Wells pursues Jack the Ripper into today's world. In the past we see and hear H.G. Wells talking about how great the future is going to be while Jack the Ripper says the opposite. However, he is very happy to arrive in

2016. The characters maintain this perspective throughout the series, and although their attitude will be challenged, it will not be exhausted.

Remember, you have characters who all want the same thing, but they'll all express how they want to achieve it differently.

Distinct Phrases

Who remembers "as if"? This phrase came into the lexicon with the premiere of the film *Clueless*. Not everyone in the movie said it—only Cher. Give your characters different catchphrases or speech patterns or give them each a specific word they constantly use.

I Saw It—You Don't Need to Say It

You're writing words for a visual medium. So if we see something happen on the screen—like a giant spaceship just landing in Citi Field—you don't have to say "A giant spaceship just landed in Citi Field!" Use the opportunity to have your characters react to it by saying something like, "Looks like the Mets team is out of this world this year."

Indirect

It's sometimes good to have indirect dialogue where the characters are figuring out what is unfolding. Maybe a woman suspects that her husband has cheated on her. She won't ask directly, though she might ask him how his day at work was.

Say the Opposite

Dialogue is sarcastic. Yep, that's right. It's always what you wish you had said ten minutes later. Have your characters quip.

Bridge Dialogue

Read the dialogue of screenwriters David Mamet or Aaron Sorkin. Characters finish each other's sentences and short words are repeated. Dialogue is bridged from one character to the other. The danger is that everyone can sound the same.

Echo Lines

"I am Groot." "Argo fuck yourself." "As if." "Round Up the Usual Suspects." There are lines that repeat in the screenplay but have different meaning as the drama builds.

It's All Work

Research the world of your story. Where does it take place? What is the environment? The profession? The Lower East Side in New York City sounds different than Silicon Valley.

Doctors and lawyers have their own terminology. If you know the world you are writing about, the dialogue will come to you.

DIALOGUE

We want you to do the **BARK** exercise.

This is designed for you to learn to write character voices because characters have different personalities and traits. Remember, the emotional DNA of a character is revealed via dialogue.

We have chosen three of the most overused lines in movies and television:

"Don't die on me, man."

"We can do this the easy way or the hard way."

"You just don't get it, do you?"

We want you to change the line to reflect the character trait listed. This will distinguish a character's voice so it is unique to their trait and personality.

For example: Let's change the line "You just don't get it, do you?" to be read by a character whose traits are "curious" and "angry."

Character trait: CURIOUS
    I imagine you had a lot of trouble understanding things as a child.

Character trait: ANGRY
    "I'm not going to tell you again."

bark exercise

TRAIT	"We can do this the easy way or the hard way."	"You just don't get it, do you?"	"Don't die on me man."
APPRECIATIVE			
CURIOUS			
PLAYFUL			
WELL-BRED			
EMOTIONAL			
SKEPTICAL			
ABRASIVE			
COWARDLY			
MONSTROUS			
THOUGHTLESS			

CHAPTER 4

Crafting Characters

WHAT COMES FIRST: PLOT OR CHARACTER?

When writing a screenplay, what comes first—*character* or *plot*? That's like asking if the chicken or the egg came first. We believe *character* comes first because from character, comes plot. Characters are about the choices they make, and these choices lead to scenes that become story. Lajos Egri, author of *The Art of Dramatic Writing: Its Basis in the Creative Interpretation of Human Motives*, said in 1946 that, "An idea will never make a story, but a character will." In this chapter, we'll show you how to create dynamic protagonists and distinctive minor characters, as well as how to best use them to enhance your script.

Let's consider the importance of character. You're going to the multiplex, and deciding on a movie. Do you say, "Let's go to that new spy thriller about a guy with amnesia who's being chased by bad guys," or do you say, "Let's go to that new *Bourne Identity* movie with Matt Damon"? You have no idea what the plot is (however, does anybody really know with the *Bourne* movies?), but you know you love the character that Matt Damon plays in the movies. We go to Melissa McCarthy and Jonah Hill movies for the characters they tend to play. Their usual characters make us laugh and feel better about life, so their plots are secondary. We go to James Bond movies over and over again—not because we really care about the plot, but because his character is a cool dude. The recent spate of Marvel movies also attests to the fact that characters are the factors that drive the box office. We can't really distinguish between the plot in *Iron Man* to its sequels, but we do know that we love his personality and his overall character.

Pole-to-Pole Transformation

Before we consider the intricacies of a character, we need to understand the broad strokes. In a movie, it's paramount that a protagonist transforms through the course of the story. Who our hero is at the beginning should be vastly different from who they are at the end. In *The Art of Dramatic Writing: Its Basis in the Creative Interpretation of Human Motives*, writer Lajos Egri refers to this transformation as the "transition" that occurs between the "poles of birth and death," which are the two vital moments of our lives. From Egri's theory, we've co-opted the term, *pole-to-pole transformation*, which we define as how the character changes from their introduction to the conclusion of the movie. When we go to the movies, we delight in seeing this transformation. In fact, it's what makes film so magical. It's not just the music or the special effects, it's knowing that unlike real life, our hero will change dramatically. Whether this means that they start out as an underdog and become a superhero, or they're a complete jerk that learns empathy by the ending, we anticipate that transformation. Actors have often said that when they're offered a part in a movie, what's critical to them is whether or not their character changes in the script. Let's consider some examples of character transformation in recent successful movies and television.

In the beginning of *Star Wars: Episode VII—The Force Awakens*, lead character Rey is an orphan scavenger who is determined to not leave her home because she's always waiting for her family to reappear. However, by the end, she's not only left her home, but she's galaxies away and has become a powerful enough warrior to fight off the evil Kylo Ren. Another lead character in the film, Finn, starts as a reluctant storm trooper blindly fighting on the side of the evil empire. By the ending, however, Finn has completely switched sides as he fights for good on the side of the Resistance.

In the animated film *Zootopia*, lead bunny Judy Hopps transforms from a naive country bumpkin to a sophisticated city cop who knows how to catch criminals and solve crimes. Judy's counterpart is Nick Wilde, a con artist fox who has given up on fairness and justice until Judy's earnestness transforms him. She makes him want to be a better person, and by doing so, he also becomes her partner on the police force.

Even in recent successful low budget movies, it's important for the character to change. Consider Susan Sarandon's character in *The Meddler*. In the beginning, she's solely focused on her daughter's life. By the ending, she's created her own life with a new boyfriend, volunteer job, and her own friends. The plot of the movie only works because we've watched the lead character change.

Movies that bomb at the box office often fail because their characters don't go through a change. Consider the recent Natalie Portman and Ewan McGregor movie, *Jane Got a Gun*. Given the magnitude of its stars, this movie should have been a hit. Instead it premiered in January of 2016, grossed less than 2 million dollars, and was dumped the same month. Granted, there is always more than one reason why a movie fails at the box office, but the story was the major culprit here and the lack of character transformation was particularly problematic. *Blog de Cine* criticized the film for not giving any depth to its characters. Another movie that failed at the box office because of its inability to demonstrate character transformation was *Phantom* (2013) starring Ed Harris and David Duchovny.

Television characters have traditionally been more static than movie characters because they are expected to go through a number of seasons with little change. But in recent successful television dramas, many of them with shorter seasons, we've seen the lead characters go through great transformations. In the beginning of *Breaking Bad*, Walter White is an honest, kind-hearted high school chemistry teacher who has cancer. By the end, he's a lying, murderous drug lord who is cancer-free.

Almost every character in *Game of Thrones* has gone through a huge transformation—especially the Stark children who were once living under the protection of their parents but are now fighting for themselves. They had to grow up sometime! And no character has changed more than Jon Snow. He went from being a bastard outcast, to a member of the Knight's Watch, to Lord Commander of The Watch. And now in season six, he's abandoned The Watch completely and there's the possibility that he might even be full Targaryen.

We can also see characters change in some recent television comedies. In *Unbreakable Kimmy Schmidt*, Kimmy is a naive thirty-five-year-old woman who has spent the last fifteen years living underground with three religious women that believe the apocalypse happened. By the end of the first season, Kimmy has traveled to New York City, moved in with a flamboyant gay man, and fallen in love. Another example is the great transformations of characters in *The Big Bang Theory*. Penny has changed from an unsuccessful actress to a wildly successful drug rep. And of course, nothing has made audiences happier than seeing Sheldon lose his virginity, finally removing the title of "virgin" from his character.

Watching characters change is what makes a story so memorable. A plot is only as good as its character's transformation.

WHAT YOUR CHARACTER NEEDS VS. WHAT THEY WANT

In addition to character transformation, we also need to understand what our character needs vs. what they want. That might sound similar, but needs and wants are vastly different. In *Shrek*, the titular character wants to get everyone out of his swamp (his home) so he can live in peace, but what he needs is love. In *Breaking Bad*, Walter White wants to make money for his family before he dies, but what he needs is power in order to consume his rage because of cancer and his job. In *Zootopia*, Judi Hopps wants to prove herself as a cop, but what she needs is love. And almost every character in D.C. Comic's *Suicide Squad* thinks they want to escape from prison, but what they really need is acceptance. Now that you understand your characters need to transform and they must have wants and needs, is it time to start writing? Not yet.

BUILDING A PROTAGONIST STEP-BY-STEP

Before you begin writing your screenplay, you need to know everything about your main character. Things like information they'd only tell their best friends to build them from the ground up. In terms of writing a movie, it's always better to have a fully developed character before moving forward with the plot. As we stated in the beginning, plot comes from character. Knowing specific quirks about our character helps us to write living, breathing characters that feel authentic. Character traits also initiate ideas for different scenes. Some of the following will sound incredibly basic and maybe even tedious at times, but these are the steps you need to follow if you want a memorable character that resonates with the reader and the audience. This list has been generated in order of most important to least important. But this is not to say that you shouldn't know how to answer all of these questions, for at least your protagonist.

NAME: Names create all kinds of connotations and the worst thing you can do is name a character something generic like Bob or Jack or Sue. In *Mad Max: Fury Road*, Charlize Theron's character is named *Imperator Furiosa*. That's a tough name and appropriate for the badass she is. *Furiosa* is also perfect because she's forever furious and willing to drive to the end of the Earth for her cause. The name Max (also in *Mad Max: Fury Road*) works well because of the alliteration in "Mad Max." Yes, he's crazy too. In the recent horror film, *It Follows*, the lead character's name is Jay. This is an interesting name because it's androgynous and makes us believe that this is something that could happen to anyone—male or female. The last name is also important. If we're looking at a light-hearted comedy like *Trainwreck*, Amy Shumer's love interest is Dr. Aaron Conners, and Conners is reminiscent of someone who cons. In this story, he's able to convince Amy, a free-spirited woman, that she can settle down and be in a monogamous relationship. TV shows especially have unique names. Look at *The Big Bang Theory*. The names Sheldon and Leonard aren't modern-day names—they both sound like old men. And in many ways, their relationship is that of two old guys who continue to live together, even after Leonard has married Penny. The name Penny also works particularly well for Kaley Cuoco's character, because in contrast to the geniuses she lives with, Penny is very simple. She's a penny among millionaires. It also goes well with, "a penny for your thoughts"—especially since Leonard is brilliant, but has no idea what Penny is thinking half the time.

AGE AND SEX: It's important to put an age on your character—at least within a decade. And typically you want to know what gender they are. However, there have been many feature films where the movie was originally meant to be a man's part, but a more bankable female actress wanted the part so it was changed. For example, take the action spy movie, *Salt*. Originally conceived as a male part, Angelina Jolie starred instead. But, as the writer, you need to indicate the character's gender in the script. And an age helps to give the reader an idea of who that person is. Here's a tip: when describing gender, be specific. Give us their age. If you say girl and you really mean a twenty-two-year-old woman, you'd better say woman. Otherwise it sounds like you're referring to an eight-year-old.

APPEARANCE: Briefly describe what the protagonist looks like. Any defects? General health? Fat or skinny? Well-dressed or untidy? A living magazine cover? Try not to say beautiful, because most actors are. Scars are interesting in films. Harry Potter's got one, and Quint (Robert Shaw) in *Jaws* compared his scars with Hooper (Richard Dreyfuss). The Joker in the *The Dark Knight*, Brad Pitt in *Inglourious Basterds,* and Inigo Montoya (Mandy Patinkin) in *The Princess Bride* had them. And, of course, there's Scar from *The Lion King*. The danger in describing a character is to say they are an "average build," "average looking," or "average height." Delete the word "average" from your screenplay! It's not specific and doesn't give us any vital information—plus no movie star wants to be considered "average"!

OCCUPATION or MAJOR: What a character does for a living, if they're a student, or what their major is tells us a lot about who they are. In *Daddy's Home*, Will Ferrell's stepdad character works for Panda, the smooth jazz radio station. This tells us right away that he's a sensitive, even-keeled guy. His antagonist, the kids' biological dad played by Mark Wahlberg, is a muscular guy. When we first meet someone, whether it's at a party, or a bar, or a classroom, the first thing we typically ask is, "What do you do?" or "What's your major?" These questions are natural ice-breakers but they're also shorthand for gaining insight on a person. Much of screenwriting is learning how to say more with less, which is why it's so important to identify a character's occupation. One last note on occupation: avoid the obvious or cliché. Avoid making your character a writer or a painter. It's just not that interesting and, most likely, it's not relatable.

ATTITUDE TOWARD LIFE: We all look at life differently even if we share the same age, sex, and occupation. Consider Will Ferrell's character in *Daddy's Home*. He's gung ho and excited about doing anything for his step-kids, even if it means he's beaten up and spending all his money. He's always an upbeat guy who's positive about life. Now consider Pat, the lead character in the recent indie hit, *The Green Room*. In the beginning, Pat is an indecisive beta-male who can't answer the simple question, "Who's your favorite desert island band?" Not that he seems suicidal, but he doesn't act like his life is worth living. Through the course of the movie he barely survives bloodcurdling dogs and lots of neo-Nazis toting guns, and by the ending he's full of life. In the very last scene, he tells his fellow survivor that he has finally figured out his desert island band. A character's attitude toward life sums up their personality.

HOBBIES: How is your character amused? Giving a character a hobby is a surefire way to avoid creating cookie-cutter characters. The hobbies work best if they're in stark contrast to the character's occupation. And sometimes the hobby ties in effectively with the plot. Consider the comedy *Knocked Up* where Paul Rudd is a successful record executive but he secretly plays fantasy baseball in the evenings. He's too embarrassed to tell his wife this, which makes her believe he's cheating on her. Without Rudd's hobby, the story misses an important plot point.

GHOST or INTERNAL PROBLEM: Every adult has at least one event from their past which haunts them. Something that still bothers them even though they might be successful and long past the failure. Often a ghost is something bad that's happened in a character's past, such as losing a parent or friend. In the television shows *Lost* and *Orange is the New Black*, we see these "ghosts" in every episode via flashbacks—but it's not necessary to use flashbacks. You can hint at something from a character's past but not have it pay off until the third act. In *Mike and Dave Need Wedding Dates*, Alice (Anna Kendrick) is haunted by her failed wedding. This is something that we view repeatedly as Alice plays her thwarted wedding video over and over on her phone. We watch as her former fiancé dumps her at the altar in the video on her phone. The "ghost" is often a major plot point that points the hero toward transformation. Alice is able to finally change when she throws away her phone.

POLE-TO-POLE TRANSFORMATION: Who is the character at the beginning and who are they at the end of the script? All of the questions about traits listed below will dovetail nicely with the *pole-to-pole transformation* of your character. If you know your character is an introvert, it's easy to see how you could show their transformation by turning them into an extrovert.

INTROVERT/EXTROVERT: Is your hero shy or outgoing? The shy underdog is a favorite protagonist among superhero movies. Consider *Spiderman* and *Batman*. Both are quiet, geeky boys with great odds against them. How they transform into superheroes and become extroverts is a fun part of the story. Female empowerment films also promote the shy woman who discovers herself. Examples are the women in *Ghostbusters* (2016) and Michelle, the female lead in *Ten Cloverfield Lane*. Conversely, a character might be an extrovert and arrogant. Watching him become humble is satisfying too. Think of Nathan Bateman, the narcissist CEO software genius who is humbled by Ava, his robotic creation in *Ex Machina*.

STRENGTHS AND VIRTUES: Give your character at least two things that they're good at. In fact, go a step farther and make them the best at one thing. Actors love to play characters that are brilliant at one thing. Consider Sheldon and all the guys on *Big Bang*. They're not just smart, they're brilliant. And even Kimmy Schmidt on *Unbreakable Kimmy Schmidt*, who might not seem like she's good at anything, is actually brilliant at making friends and making people happy.

FAULTS AND WEAKNESSES: If a character is completely perfect, they're not going to be likeable or relatable—we've all got flaws, so don't forget to give them to your characters. Flaws work especially well in comedies. Think about Will Ferrell again in *Daddy's Home* (and actually any movie he's in)—he's a flabby guy without much strength, meaning he definitely can't build a tree house like his nemesis Mark Wahlberg does. But his flaws make him hilarious. Also consider the *Hangover* movies. We love watching Zach Galifianakis because he's so flawed.

CLASS IN SOCIETY: Is your character "working class"? "White collar"? "Blue collar"? The top 1 percent? Once you know that, could you move to another class, or is it even important? In *Slumdog Millionaire*, the lead character's lower class status triggers the plot of the movie. If the main character had been from an upper class, no one would have questioned his ability to be so brilliant on a game show.

EDUCATION LEVEL: It's important to know how many years of school your hero has attended and perhaps even what college they've attended, if they've attended college. Is it a state university or an Ivy League? In *The Big Bang Theory*, Sheldon and Leonard rib Howard Wolowitz for his engineering degree because they consider it to be lowbrow next to their PhD. In *Good Will Hunting*, Matt Damon's character is a brilliant mathematician who just happens to be the janitor at Harvard and not a student. The fact that he's never attended college, yet he's far more intelligent than the Ivy League grads he cleans up after, is what makes him such a fascinating character.

HOME LIFE: In *Good Will Hunting*, Matt Damon's character was abused in multiple foster care situations, which led him to have an inability to trust people. The character of Harry Potter was forged partly by his home life, where he grew up unwanted and was forced to sleep in a closet under the stairs. A character's home life also creates opportunities for his pole-to-pole transformation. Harry Potter went from being an unloved orphan to a well-liked student with a tightly-knit group of friends who became his family. In *Star Wars: Episode VII—The Force Awakens*, Rey was also an orphan. It's interesting to note that we often see movie characters who have had crummy childhoods. They are often missing one or both parents. Why? Because it helps to create more conflict in life. We'd all love to have perfect lives, but easy lives don't make for interesting movies.

LOVE LIFE and SEX LIFE: Does your character have a love life or sex life? Have they recently gone through a breakup? Did they do the breaking up or were they dumped? In the *Bridget Jones' Diary* movies, Bridget is forever falling in and out of love and has trouble with her sex life, but in the third movie of this trilogy, the story takes this complication to a new level. Bridget has sex with the two men in her life, and when she becomes pregnant, she's not sure who the father is. Thus trouble ensues.

PERSONAL AMBITION: What is your character's personal ambition? If the answer to this question is none, then why do they lack personal ambition? What happened in their life to make them give up? Conversely, if they're an ambitious type A personality, what drives them? In *The Wolf of Wall Street* and the more recent Jonah Hill movie, *War Dogs*, we meet men who grew up in the middle class but are desperate to be in the top 1 percent. Their driving ambition also drives the plot. In contrast, the characters that lack drive in the beginning of a film can be frustrating, but they can also set in motion that pole-to-pole transformation as we see their characters change.

FRUSTRATIONS/CHIEF DISAPPOINTMENTS IN LIFE: Going back to uninteresting characters with perfect lives, consider what kinds of things your hero regrets. What would they have done differently if they'd had the chance?

CHILDHOOD AND CURRENT DREAMS: What did your character want to be when they were a child? Did that dream change? If it did, what's the dream now? If we know our character's dreams, we know what their goals are. Every good character needs to be reaching toward something.

COMPLEXITIES, OBSESSIONS, INHIBITIONS, SUPERSTITIONS, PHOBIAS: What are your character's complexities? Just in case it hasn't been covered thus far, you need to know what drives your character crazy with obsession; what scares or inhibits them, what are their superstitions, and/ or what are their phobias?

RACE/NATIONALITY: It's true that you can certainly write so that the part you are creating can be played by anybody. But if your story calls for a specific ethnicity, don't shy away from including it in the script. A movie like *Straight Outta Compton* is a movie that deals with race in Los Angeles at the emergence of hip-hop.

PLACE IN THE COMMUNITY: Is your character on the hospital board? An elected official? A shopkeeper? In the television show *Friday Night Lights*, Coach was the most popular and hated man in the community based on how the team performed.

POLITICS: Is your character liberal? Conservative? Libertarian? Independent? Or do they not care? *House of Cards* is all about this.

RELIGION: While religion plays a smaller part in most movies today, it might be important for your character. Whether they're Buddhist, Christian, Jewish, Muslim, or another faith, it might inform how they act. A show like *The Leftovers* is all about religion and faith and questioning the big "What If's."

EXTERNAL PROBLEM: Your character's external problem is the last thing to consider because it's the most closely linked to the plot of your story. Once you know everything about your character, it will be easy to know what problem they might encounter. This problem will then become the inciting incident, or the plot point that causes the movie to turn in a new direction—and that's when your story really begins. Think about a movie like *Shrek*—his external problem is rid his swamp of the fairy tale creatures. He achieves his goal but finds out it's not what he wanted after all.

In *Star Wars: The Force Awakens*, Rey wants to find her family. But her external problem has to do with saving BB-8 and finding Luke Skywalker.

Now that you've created this exhaustive list for your protagonist, you probably know more about them than you do about your best friend or even yourself! It's safe to say that it's time to move past the protagonist and figure out who the rest of the characters are in your movie.

Writing Multiple Characters Using the Four Elements

Movies typically have more than one character because the protagonist needs to be in conflict with another person. Exceptions include the movies with plotlines of man vs. nature such as *127 Hours*, which is when James Franco's protagonist gets stuck in a crevice and we wait two hours to see if he's going to free himself or die. In *The Shallows*, Blake Lively's character is alone for most of the movie as she battles it out against a shark. But most movies have other characters rounding out the story. And this is where it can be challenging because when we write a scene, it's paramount that the characters are distinctive from each other. Not only should they look different, they need to act and speak differently. Even members of the same family can and should be different from each other. This can be daunting, but there are tricks you can use.

One of our favorite ways to flesh out a scene with distinctive characters is to look at the four elements, Earth, Wind, Fire, and Water. Now, what if we had four characters in a scene, and each person represented one of these elements? To start, you need to create a list of adjectives that define each element. Here's how we'd do it: Our *Earth* character is grounded, level-headed, sensible, and pragmatic. Examples include Groot from *Guardians of the Galaxy* and almost any mother in a movie. Our *Wind* character is mercurial, empty, pompous, and boastful. Examples of these characters are Nathan Bateman in *Ex Machina* and any villain in a superhero movie. Our *Fire* character is passionate, destructive, enthusiastic, and spontaneous and any character in *Suicide Squad* would be a great example. Our *Water* character is peaceful, transparent, fluid, and weak. An example of this is Caleb in *Ex Machina*.

Just by using these elements, we have instantly created four vibrantly different personalities, thereby making our scene more interesting. For more examples, consider the Academy Award winning screenplay, *Little Miss Sunshine*. The little girl and the mother were the Earth. The father and the grandfather were the Wind. The uncle was the Fire. The brother was the Water.

The last, best thing you can do is: Keep It Real. Base your characters on people you know. Especially family. You know the world you live in, make it the world you write in. If you have a crazy sister who does crazy things, put her in your story. We once based an evil character on a relative. The movie got made. The phone rang. It was that relative. We were worried. The relative was going to hate us. Turns out that character was their favorite character in the movie. They had no idea.

The Antagonist

Now go back and build your protagonist. Pretend they are the hero of the story. Yes, the antagonist is the villain. The bad guy or girl. The dark side. But if you asked the antagonist why are they are so mean, they would be confounded.

A well-crafted antagonist is a character who believes they are doing the right thing. Lady Macbeth urges Macbeth on to kill and be king because she thinks that they will rule better than all. Macbeth believes the prophecy is real. In *X-Men: First Class,* we see the origin of Magneto. He has been captive in a concentration camp and has watched his mother die. He was experimented on, manipulated. All of his actions are from his primal need of revenge. He does not trust humans and wants to protect his mutants. He does not believe the two can co-exist.

Yet sometimes the villain can just be a force of hell. In *No Country for Old Men,* Javier Barden as Anton Chigurh is this type of villain. He is a monster. Yet he has a code. He takes his job seriously and when he flips a coin to decide if someone will live or die, he honors that. If you ask Anton, he would say he is a principled man of honor.

The antagonist has the qualities we have renounced. It sometimes helps to think of the antagonist as the mirror of your hero; the persona that he or she is petrified of becoming. The antagonist is dedicated to death or the destruction of things, relationships, jobs. Or in a comedy—it just might be Biff, as in the *Back to the Future* series. He is Marty's antagonist throughout time.

Take a look at the American Film Institute's 100 Greatest Heroes and Villains.[1] Each villain has a clear motivation. Norman Bates in *Psycho* loves his mother (too much). Even the alien in *Alien* has an instinctual, evolutionary reason to kill to survive. In *The Conjuring,* Bathsheba is a witch whose spirit takes over humans who sacrificed her week-old child to the devil and then killed herself in 1863 after cursing all who would take her land. They find reports of numerous murders and suicides in houses that had since been built on the property.[2]

Antagonists need to have motivation. They believe the story is happening to them. You should be able to tell the story from the antagonist's point of view. In *Ferris Bueller's Day Off*, there's a reason Principal Rooney is hell-bent on catching Ferris. He has failed to do so in the past.

Antagonists do not have to be people. The antagonist of the story can be a shark or a whale. We see this occur in *Jaws, The Shallows,* and *In the Heart of the Sea.* It can be a disease such as mental illness in *A Beautiful Mind.* Comedies might make the antagonist a curse—as in *Groundhog Day* and *Liar Liar.* In romantic comedies it might be the person that he or she is falling in love with.

Bottom line: make your villains human. Give us a reason to hate them but also more reasons to like them. Hannibal Lecter is one of the most famous villains of all time (from the novel, movies, and television show). He is a cannibal. Yet he loves good food, good music; he is an artist and he also has a need to protect Clarice. He is cultivated, cunning, and clever, but never forget he eats liver with a nice Chianti.

ENDNOTES

1. http://www.afi.com/100Years/handv.aspx

2. https://en.wikipedia.org/wiki/The_Conjuring

CRAFTING CHARACTER

Using the questions we asked in Chapter Four, we are going to build the main character for your screenplay. As you do this, you will start generating scene ideas that you can use to craft your stories. We are looking for character-driven stories with character-driven scenes. You will be using these scenes as you structure the screenplay—short or long.

In the "Idea Space" write down a scene idea based on the "Answers" for your character.

EXAMPLE: in *Knocked Up*, Pete's (Paul Rudd) hobby is fantasy baseball. That became a hilarious (SPOILER ALERT) scene where Debbie (Leslie Mann) tracks him down to the house where she thinks he's having an affair, but he's actually playing fantasty baseball with a group of guys.

build a character

QUESTIONS	ANSWERS	IDEA SPACE
NAME		
AGE & SEX		
APPEARANCE Physical Description		

CONTINUE TO NEXT PAGE

build a character

QUESTIONS	ANSWERS	IDEA SPACE
APPEARANCE Emotional Description		
OCCUPATION OR MAJOR		
ATTITUDE TOWARDS LIFE		

CONTINUE TO NEXT PAGE

build a character

QUESTIONS	ANSWERS	IDEA SPACE
HOBBIES		
GHOST or INTERNAL PROBLEM		
POLE-TO-POLE TRANSFORMATION		

CONTINUE TO NEXT PAGE

build a character

QUESTIONS	ANSWERS	IDEA SPACE
INTROVERT/ EXTROVERT		
STRENGTHS & VIRTUES		
CLASS IN SOCIETY		

CONTINUE TO NEXT PAGE

build a character

QUESTIONS	ANSWERS	IDEA SPACE
EDUCATION LEVEL		
HOME LIFE		
LOVE LIFE/ SEX LIFE		

CONTINUE TO NEXT PAGE

build a character

QUESTIONS	ANSWERS	IDEA SPACE
PERSONAL AMBITION		
FRUSTRATIONS/ DISAPPOINTMENTS IN LIFE		
CHILDHOOD & CURRENT DREAMS		

CONTINUE TO NEXT PAGE

build a character

QUESTIONS	ANSWERS	IDEA SPACE
COMPLEXITIES, OBSESSIONS, INHIBITIONS, SUPERSTITIONS, PHOBIAS		
RACE/NATIONALITY		
POLITICS & RELIGION		

CHAPTER 5

Writing the Scene

So how do you actually write a script? How does it go from an idea, onto a page, and finally into a movie, TV show, or short film? A comparison might be to ask yourself how a house is built. A house doesn't just appear unless it's *The Wizard of Oz*. A house has to be designed carefully and then constructed one piece of wood at a time. Screenplays are similar: screenwriters design the house, then build it.

You write the script by writing scene by scene. Each scene adds to the overall construction of the screenplay. You can't add scenes if you don't know what they're going to be about or how they fit into the framework of the story.

As the writer outlines and builds their story, they must look ahead and decide what needs to go into each scene. You have to know what the characters want and what you, as a writer, want the scene to accomplish. Is this the scene where the audience laughs, or the one where they jump out of their seats?

This is why outlining is so important. However, you can't really outline until you know how scenes work. Writing for the screen is elliptical: one scene forward, two scenes back.

We want to take you through what makes a scene work. If you can get into a pattern where one event leads to the next, you have a chance at keeping the audience's interest.

SCENE INTERROGATION—TEN QUESTIONS TO ASK YOUR SCENE

Here are a series of questions to consider for every scene in your story. As you develop your story and assemble your story points, interrogate your script. Be tough with the script as well as on yourself. It will make you a better writer.

1. DOES YOUR SCENE KEEP US IN THE STORY?

We want scenes that belong in the movie or, rather, scenes that often relate to the theme that holds the whole thing together. We call this the spine. This is not to say that every scene needs to be wholly dramatic in a drama. Instead, you want moments of levity in a drama and, conversely, just a touch of drama in a comedy. You don't want scenes that remove us from the main story, characters, or the tone of the piece. For example, in *500 Days of Summer*, Tom (Joseph Gordon Levitt) is in love and suddenly starts singing a full musical number in a park. This film is ripe with fantastical tropes that make the scene feel as if it belongs within the course of the story. However, if a similar scene was placed in *Sully*, where Captain Sully starts singing and dancing, it would seem like a different movie. In the classic *Butch Cassidy and the Sundance Kid*, there is a bike ride montage set to the song "Raindrops Keep Falling On My Head" where the relationships between Butch, Sundance, and Etta is extrapolated on. It reveals character: Butch is always looking to the future but at the end of the scene he lets the bike fall to the ground. The tone is foreboding—telling the audience that these men don't have a future.

2.   DOES THE SCENE ADVANCE THE STORY?

We hate the "unrated" or the special edition cuts of a movie. Movies are written three times: you write them, film them, and then edit. Stories need to keep moving. This is why scenes are cut out in the editing process. You need to do the same thing in your script by going through each scene and seeing if that scene advances the action of the story. The plot should advance through the events of the dramatic action and some new plot twist should occur, causing the next scene to happen. Everything after the inciting incident (see Structure chapter) is cause and effect. Trey Parker and Matt Stone (co-creators of *South Park*) famously crashed a screenwriting class and told students that all you need to know are the words "therefore" and "but." Think of these words when constructing your overall story. Something happens (A SCENE) so THEREFORE something else happens (another SCENE), BUT something spins the story into the unexpected. The story should have a back and forth of "therefore" and "but." In television, the "but" might come just before the commercial break.

3.   DOES THE SCENE OPEN A CHARACTER WINDOW?

Scenes also need to open character windows—or rather, they must give the audience a little insight into the character. In the beginning of the story, you open the window just a crack. Toward the end of the series or movie, that window is opened wider revealing more and more of the character. In the movie *Guardians of the Galaxy*, there is a scene where Rocket Raccoon is about to get into a brawl. In his drunken rage, Rocket talks about what a freak he is because he was experimented upon. Through this, we learn a lot more about this sad, angry, yet funny raccoon. Characters' windows are revealing. They show us backstories that bring us closer to the characters.

4.   DOES YOUR SCENE HAVE CLEAR IMPLICATIONS AND LIKELY REPERCUSSIONS?

Do you know what you want out of a scene? Do the characters know what they want, and if they don't get it, are there implications? Are they conflicted? It's always good to place your characters in a position of choice. In the landmark *Sopranos* episode "College," Tony takes his daughter, Meadow, on a tour of colleges and it's his proudest moment. For all the immoral things he has done in his life, Tony can look at himself in the rearview mirror and see that, in spite of his flaws, he managed to do well in raising his daughter. She has a future that is bright. But then, Tony sees an old colleague who is now in the Witness Protection Program after testifying against the family. Tony has to choose what to do—be a father or a mobster. Tony drops Meadow off at school and goes off to kill the old colleague. It was a defining moment in the series because it showed that Tony was never going to let go of the evil side of himself, no matter how much he loved being a parent.

5.   DOES THE SCENE HAVE CONFLICT?

Television is wonderful. We know this because of iconic shows like *All in the Family, M*A*S*H, The Twilight Zone,* and *Seinfeld.* One of the most beloved shows—and a show that has been around for fifty years—is *Star Trek.* The first series (The Original Series or TOS) was amazing. It was one of the most diverse, reflective shows in terms of casting and it was one of the first shows that dealt with what was going on in our world at the time—things such as world wars, cold wars, overpopulation. The conflict between Kirk, Spock, and McCoy was always present as they agreed to disagree on whatever was happening on the show.

When *Star Trek* was rebooted as *Star Trek: The Next Generation* in 1987, Gene Roddenberry, the creator of the original *Star Trek,* wanted to correct a few problems he saw in the original series. As reported in the documentary, *Chaos on the Bridge,* which was written and directed by William Shatner (who played Captain Kirk in *Star Trek*), Roddenberry didn't like the Kirk/Spock/McCoy conflict of the first series, and believed that there should be no conflict on the bridge of the next generation. Writers knew that this was a terrible idea, but had to execute it anyway. They did the no-conflict starship as well as anyone could, but basically, there was no way to do it. Writers came and went. The series didn't really "click" until Picard became a Borg in season three. You always need conflict.

The best conflict between characters occurs when each character believes they are right. You have to be able to justify both sides of the argument. As a writer, you also need to be able to tap into the darkness of your soul to write that dark destroyer character.

Nothing should come easy for your protagonist, so each scene should have internal conflict (ties in with the character arc) and external conflict (keeps the story interesting).

Internal conflict is the something that is bothering the main character. Something they carry with them. Jon Snow from *Game of Thrones* is the bastard child of the Stark House, so he never feels like a Stark. He carries this with him through most of the series. He slowly changes because that is what TV is like—a slow burn.

The external conflict is that everyone wants the throne and Jon is often engaged in a battle for his life.

In the British import, *Catastrophe*, airing on Amazon, the comedy is ripe with internal and external conflicts. The leads, played by Sharon Horgan and Rob Delany, constantly banter and argue at hysterical proportions. Sharon did not want to become pregnant and Rob did not want to have to move to Britain—plus he's an alcoholic, giving him internal conflict as well. The external conflict comes from whatever is happening in their lives: problems with family, friends, and work, as well as complications with the pregnancy. The genius in the show is that pretty much everything in life is a catastrophe, yet they manage to get through it.

6.   *IS THE SCENE IN THE MOMENT?*

Screenwriting is making pieces of a puzzle fit. You can't just open the box and go start putting the pieces together; you work in sections. Say you're assembling a puzzle of a giant steamboat passing the Statue of Liberty—you might start with the green of the statue or the hull of the boat. And that is what you worry about—that section.

In *Guardians of the Galaxy*, our heroes have to save the galaxy but can't do so without breaking out of prison first. They live in the moment of getting out—so to us, the overall plot doesn't matter. The task in front of them is the most important thing at that moment.

In *Spotlight*, the reporters look for connections and information, hoping that one interview might lead to another.

In *No Country For Old Men*, Llewelyn Moss (played by Josh Brolin) makes the decision to bring water to a dying man. It leads to a lot of trouble, but in that moment, it's the only task on his mind.

Characters need to have a goal that will help them get to the larger goal of the story. Stories are about people who want a certain thing as well as the obstacles that stand in their way. Scenes are the same way.

For each scene, consider this: What do your characters want specifically right now, and what do they want in the long-term?

In the movie *Sully*, Sully wants to land a plane. He doesn't want his reputation and name cleared—that comes later.

In *Deadpool*, Deadpool wants his face and the love of his life back, but to do that, he needs to cause a lot of mayhem along the way. And grow a new hand.

In *Zootopia*, Judy Hopps wants to be a police-rabbit even though that has never happened in the history of Zootopia. Her overall objectives differ from her immediate goal, and those goals build as the story builds. Judy goes from writing tickets to realizing her dreams.

In *Suicide Squad*, the squad has no real goal. It shifts. First it's a rescue, and then it's saving the world. We're not sure what was happening.

In *The Martian*, botanist Mark Watney wants to get home. To do that he has to stay alive and grow potatoes by building a greenhouse, mixing his own excrements with soil, and find a way to get water. He doesn't have time to worry about the getting home part when first he has to get water from a rock! Each of the tasks he undertakes is a scene, thereby each has an immediate goal. Yes, he succeeds at all of them, but it is never easy. There are setbacks galore. Everything you want in the scene will evolve organically from what the characters want, and nothing is more organic than growing potatoes on Mars.

Let's look at the television show, *Stranger Things*. As they search for their missing friend Will, Dustin, Mike, and Lucas find "E" (Eleven) walking in the woods. Their overall goal is to find their friend, but as the scene progresses, they realize "E" might be able to help them. Their immediate goal changes, as does the following scene goals. They need to hide, feed, and communicate with "E."

Each scene is a smaller objective. If that smaller objective is out of reach, the overall objective might not be achievable either. Usually the current objective is not met or it spins into an unexpected direction. This takes us to the next scene of the story. And onward and onward . . .

7.   *WHAT IN THE SCENE IS VISUALLY INTERESTING?*

Screenwriting is not playwriting. A playwright will tell you where the table is positioned on the stage in relationship to the bedroom set. Screenwriting is about writing words for moving pictures rather than a live audience watching live actors. Visual information is always best in screenplays because it is a visual medium. Movies used to rule when it came to being visually interesting, and they still do. Television does not come close to the wide-screen spectacle that a summer blockbuster can pull off. Although, TV has gotten better and is considered more "cinematic" than ever. This change is attributed to wide-screen television monitors being purchased in most homes. Cinematographers have taken advantage of this on shows like *Game of Thrones, Sons of Anarchy,* and *Breaking Bad.* The quality of the production matches the quality of the writing. *Downtown Abbey* was a wonderful series that was filmed beautifully. Everything upstairs was civilized and the camera was on a tripod with static shots. But once we went downstairs, the camera was free-floating or handheld, reflecting the kinetic and hectic energy that was the life of the servants. Most television, especially broadcast television is stuck in "walk and talk and sit" mode. People standing around a room talking about the plot, moving it forward, and then dealing with the fallout.

Writers need to find a way to write visually. We tell students that they should give us three images in the scene description before any action takes place. Dirty dishes. A dripping sink. An empty scotch bottle. These might be the three images that set up a good introduction to a character.

Remember that action is character. In the opening scene of *Whiplash,* we see Andrew (Miles Teller) playing drums. He is alone and exhausted. This shows us how hard he is willing to work on his craft. This follows the rule of showing, not telling, to convey information about a character. Then Fletcher (J.K. Simmons) appears and is intrigued as he listens. He tests Andrew and Andrew fails (intimacy through failure bonds us to the character). When Andrew looks up, Fletcher is gone. He is devastated because he lost an important opportunity—but then the scene turns when Fletcher walks back in. He retrieves his coat and leaves again. Andrew is crushed, but never has to say a word about it because of the visual communication of these feelings to the audience.

8. IS THE SCENE STRUCTURED CORRECTLY?

Scene structure = screenplay structure. There is a beginning, middle, and end to each scene you write.

Beginning of a Scene: pulls us in and presents a problem; somebody wants something.

Middle of Scene: addresses the consequences of the problem; action leads to reaction.

End of Scene: conclusion or any unexpected scene which leads to a "Now what?" moment.

9. DOES YOUR SCENE HAVE THE FIVE W'S?

Exposition is important to story. The audience needs to know some sort of background to get involved in the story. When it comes to delivering exposition, a scene is always more interesting when a character needs to work for and find a way to get information rather than when it's simply given to them. Please don't subscribe to exposition TV or radio. This is when a character turns on a television and everything anyone needs to know about the plot is told to us right there, at the perfect time.

Exposition also might contain any of the following five W's:

WHO is the scene about? Stories are about people who want things and the obstacles that stand in their way. New writers don't change point-of-view enough. Every scene has the protagonist leading the scene. Just because there are stars for movies or the TV shows does not mean that *every* scene has to be from their point-of-view. Look at television. *Lost* told stories from Jack, Kate, Sawyer, Locke, and many other characters' points-of-view. For each scene, ask yourself: What do your characters want right now versus long-term?

WHAT happens in the scene? What is the action and how are you choosing to write it? What are you showing us? Remember that you're writing for a visual medium, so you need to visualize each moment of choice for the characters.

WHERE is the scene taking place? Most television shows have three main locations. The crew builds each of these sets, and during the story, the characters bounce between the three rooms to discuss what is happening. However, in shows like *Battlestar Galactica,* we see different worlds, and not just other planets, but the environment in which humans are surviving as well as the environment where Cylons reside.

WHEN is the scene taking place? Is the time of year important? Can you build the scene around holidays or a birthday? It's amazing how many great movies have life-changing scenes during a "When" that the audience can relate to.

WHY does something happen in the scene? Sometimes it's not because of the plot, but rather it's because of the story and the theme. Plot is there for the character to change, so are they affected by what is happening? Protagonists are reluctant to change, but scenes where they have to make a choice help them get there.

10.   IS THE SCENE ENTERTAINING?

The ultimate goal for any script is to entertain. It is the entertainment business after all. For each scene you should be able to elicit an emotion from the viewer and indifference is not an emotion. You want to write scenes that the audience will watch and lean closer to the screen or sit straight up in their seats. You should have an idea of the EMOTIONAL EVENT you want to occur in each scene, like revelations and reactions. In *The Americans*, we learn early on that their next-door neighbor and friend is an FBI agent.

Writers have their own objective. The writer's objective is to write for the audience, not themselves. Of course, you should have a thematic reason to write the story, but you're not writing haikus. You are writing for an industry that wants people consuming content in theaters or on their couches. We're hoping that it's content you created. That audience wants to be entertained. We think new screenwriters fail when they don't involve the audience.

Sometimes you have to forget the character's objective and realize that the writer's objective is just as important. The writer knows that they have to manipulate the audience because it is their job to influence their emotions. It is also the writer's objective to keep the show on the air, otherwise they don't get paid.

To manipulate the audience, the writer has to include scenes that keep them involved. The famous director Alfred Hitchcock (*Psycho, North by Northwest, Notorious*) was known as the master of suspense, not the master of the surprise. A scene that shocks the audience with something unexpected might have the viewer involved in the story for a few seconds, but if you devise a scene or a series of scenes where the audience is leaning forward at the edge of their seat, it might be minutes of screen time where audiences are engaged with the story.

In *Breaking Bad*, we know that Walter is a drug dealer and his brother-in-law Hank is the law enforcement agent in charge of bringing him down. Every scene with Walter and Hank has underlying tension.

In the very smart semi-sequel *10 Cloverfield Lane*, Michelle has been kidnapped by Howard. She is stuck with another man, Emmet. Howard tells them that the world has been invaded, but how do we know that's the truth? The audience wants to know and clues are revealed throughout the film. When Emmet takes a "Breaking Bad" bath (spoiler), it becomes clear that Michelle is in a lot of trouble. She manages to escape the bunker only to see that Howard *was* telling the truth. Michelle stands on a car, watches an alien spaceship fly overhead, and curses the situation. The audience reacts to this because they were with her every step of the way.

Richard Donner did not want to direct the 1978 *Superman*. He only did so after figuring out the heart of the story: a love triangle between two people—Clark and Superman and Lois. He also knew he had to tap into the Frank "Capra-corn" America and cast the iconic Glenn Ford as Jonathan Kent. Jonathan knows that Clark was not brought to this planet to catch footballs and believes that his son will do good in the world. He is an optimistic. When he dies, Clark is as heartbroken as the audience.

In the reboot entitled *Man of Steel* (2013), the role of Jonathan is played by Kevin Costner. Costner is as American as they come because of his past career in baseball movies (*Field of Dreams, Bull Durham*) and American hero movies (*JFK, The Untouchables*). And of course, let's not forget his Oscar-winning performance in *Dances with Wolves*. It's perfect casting for Clark Kent's Dad.

But perfect casting does not win over imperfect writing. The creative team behind *Man of Steel* got everything wrong. Jonathan warns his son never to reveal his powers. So when Clark asks if he should have just let a bus of school children die, Jonathan basically says yes. In the 1978 *Superman*, Clark would have done everything in his power to save Pa Kent, but in the end, he couldn't. In *Man of Steel*, Clark is ordered by his father not to save him from a deadly tornado, so in the end Clark has to watch his father die.

This storyline is pure torture for the character *and* the audience. The 1978 death of Pa Kent is earned and leads to other choices and stories that influence Clark's desire to help people either as a reporter or Superman. The *Man of Steel* Pa Kent death made the filmmakers lose the audience because they were wondering what was happening and why.

Death in movies has to be earned or lead to something. Audiences don't demand a happy ending but they want a satisfying ending. They constantly want HOPE AND FEAR in the scenes. They HOPE one thing will happen but FEAR it will. Jack and Rose both don't survive the Titanic.

Acclaimed screenwriter Richard Price (*The Color of Money, Sea of Love*) wrote, "The way I learned was by watching movies and pretending I was the writer of what I was seeing."[1]

When we first broke in to Hollywood it was because of a script we had written that attracted the attention of producer Gary Foster (*Community*). Gary wanted to try to set up our screenplay at a studio but thought that we needed some more "trailer scenes."

"What's a trailer scene?" we asked.

"Don't you lie in bed at night and dream about seeing your movie trailer on the big screen? What scenes would they be showing?"

We answered that we had never done that before.

"You should."

And so should you . . .

ENDNOTE

1. 3 Screenplays, Richard Price.

SCENE WRITING

A good way to improve your scene writing is to break down a scene from an existing movie or TV show.

Here's how we suggest you do it:

1. Find a scene you enjoy from a TV show and a movie.

2. Break the scene into beats. That means each time something happens, you write it down.

3. By the end of the 2–3 minute scene, you should have about 5–7 beats.

4. Then next to each beat, rate it as either a positive event, a negative event, or a neutral event. You'll notice how a positive beat followed by a negative beat creates conflict in the scene and often turning points which is exactly how you keep your scenes from being dull and one note.

5. Then identify the beats according to one of these structure points listed below. Every scene needs to have these beats in order to keep it interesting and worthwhile for the script: SETUP—INCITING EVENT—CONFLICT—TURNING POINTS—UNEXPECTED

USE THE WORKSHEET ON THE NEXT PAGE TO IDENTIFY THE BEATS IN YOUR STORY.

scene worksheet

RISING ACTION:

What is happening to the characters BEFORE the scene begins.
Are they in a good mood (positive) or bad mood (negative)?

WHO WANTS WHAT IN THE SCENE?

_____   _____

_____   _____

_____   _____

WHAT IS THE OBSTACLE?

Is it a Person? A Place or a Thing?

LIST THE BEATS OF A SCENE:

_____   _____

_____   _____

_____   _____

DO THE BEATS BUILD?

WHAT IS THE TURNING POINT OF THE SCENE?

_____

_____

HOW DOES THE SCENE CHANGE THE CHARACTER OR ADVANCE THE PLOT?

_____

_____

CHAPTER

What Is Structure?

The screenwriter William Goldman (*Marathon Man, Butch Cassidy and the Sundance Kid, All the President's Men, The Princess Bride*) wrote in his acclaimed book *Adventures in the Screen Trade*, "Screenplays are Structure."

As structure is so important to all short films we first want to present an overview of structure. In later chapters we will discuss the nuances of short film structure and feature film structure.

Spoiler Alert

Before reading this chapter, please watch the following short films on YouTube:

> *Doodlebug, Black Hole, Gridlock, Lunch Date,* and *Consent.* This will enhance your reading of this chapter on structure.

THREE ACTS: THEY'RE LIKE FEATURE FILMS, BUT SHORTER

Unlike playwriting and other forms of writing, screenwriting is a relatively new form of storytelling. Movies didn't even exist until the movie camera was invented in the late 1800s. The first patented film camera was designed in 1888 by Louis Le Prince.[1] And given that the "talkies" weren't made until 1927 with *The Jazz Singer*, the form of screenwriting as we know it has been around for less than a hundred years. In contrast, playwriting dates back to the Greeks in the fourth century BC.

Bear with us for a very brief history lesson here. Aristotle's *Poetics* (from that fourth century we were talking about) is considered to be the first playwriting manual. It's still used today by both playwrights and screenwriters. *Poetics* established the importance of action as the basis for all drama (Poetics). It also stresses plot, character, and the importance of a conflict-driven story.

Aristotle is best known for clarifying that "a tragedy needs a beginning, middle, and end," but he never referred to it as a three-act structure.[2]

After Aristotle, the next important playwriting instruction came from the Roman theorist Horace (65–8 BC), who declared that plays must have a five-act structure. His rules were followed for 2,000 years until the eighteenth century. Then, in the late eighteenth and early nineteenth century, the popular playwrights Pixérécourt and Kotzebue were credited with the development of "melodrama," which early silent film utilized to spectacular effect. But it was the playwright Scribe whom first wowed audiences with the intensified use of action.[3]

Gustav Freytag is credited with writing the first modern playwriting manual, *Technique of the Drama* in 1863. Freytag emphasized pragmatic guidelines as opposed to arbitrary rules (Freytag, 1863). It's noteworthy that many of the screenwriting terms that we use now were first mentioned in Freytag's book. These terms include *controlling idea, cause and effect,* and *rising action.* Furthermore, one of the most important structural beats in screenwriting today is the moment in the first act when the plot initially turns in a new direction. Today this is typically referred to as the inciting incident, the point of attack, or the catalyst. Freytag called it the exciting force.[4] In her 2012 *Screentakes* article, "A History of Three-Act Structure," Jennine Lanouette writes, "Freytag's greatest influence was through what has come to be known as 'Freytag's pyramid,' which is a graphic representation of rising and falling action in the shape of an isosceles triangle."[5] On this graph, Freytag charts five parts to the action, with the climax occurring squarely in the middle at the highest peak of the pyramid. He carefully avoids the word "act," with its connotation as an arbitrary segment of scenes. Nonetheless, his five-part thinking indicates that he has not yet broken free of the five-act dictates of Horace.

In 1912, William Archer published *Play-making,* an instructional text that focused on a three-act structure instead of the five-act model. Archer included many of the screenwriting terms that we use today such as *point of attack, preparation, obstacle, crisis, climax,* and *denouement* (*Play-making,* by William Archer, 1912). With the advent of moviemaking in the late 1800s, there were a few manuals on screenwriting that cropped up but they focused on technique as opposed to story. These early manuals were designed for the director, with lists of shots and scenes included.

Then in 1936, John Howard Lawson wrote the first instructional text that focused on the storytelling aspect of screenwriting. The book was titled *Theory and Technique of Playwriting and Screenwriting.* Like Archer, Lawson discussed cycles of action but he didn't refer to structure in terms of acts. It wasn't until 1939 that we see the three-act structure fully embraced in Kenneth Rowe's book, *Write that Play.* Rowe writes, "Three movements are clearly more basic to the fundamental structure of a dramatic action than Horace's five. There is an attack, a crisis, and a resolution" (Rowe, *Write that Play,* 1939).

There have been many screenwriting texts over the years but none have been quite as popular as those written by the legendary screenwriting guru, Syd Field. His first book was *Screenplay: The Foundations of Screenwriting* (1979). In this book, Syd Field created the paradigm that we still use today, which includes three acts and the specific sections that go with each act. Act One and Act Three are of the same length in terms of pages and Act Two is double the length of either. In terms of page lengths, Act One and Act Three are defined as having thirty pages or being thirty minutes long, give or take. Act Two is sixty pages, which equates to about sixty minutes long. Then Syd Field went beyond the three-act structure to suggest a four-act structure, which included Act One, Act Two-A, Act Two-B, and Act Three. Field stresses the importance of the midpoint that occurs between Act Two-A and Act Two-B. His act structure is the paradigm that we prefer to use when writing and teaching about structure. In conclusion, screenwriters of today owe much to the dramatists of the past centuries.

WHAT IS STRUCTURE?

At its core, structure refers to how we organize the scenes in a movie. Because we're not beholden to a stage, and we can jump around in time and space, we can do literally whatever we want. This presents both the exciting and challenging aspects of screenwriting.

In the broadest terms, Act One includes the setup and introduction of the problem for the protagonist.

Act Two includes the protagonist trying to solve that problem.

Act Three has the protagonist finally solving the problem.

Even the shortest of short films follow this three-act structure. What's different is that the structure in a short film is truncated in certain beats compared to that of a feature.

Unlike a feature, Act One of a short film ends with the inciting incident. The term "inciting incident" refers to the plot point that's introduced that will create a problem for the hero and will upset his normal life. It's the story point that turns our movie in a new direction. This incident should be a dramatic problem that's worthy of forcing our hero to want to solve the crisis that's been thrown at him. If the inciting incident is too small, our hero won't care and the reader/viewer won't care either. And if that happens, the reader puts down the script and the viewer turns off the movie or leaves the theatre.

Act Two often begins with the hero in denial as he refuses to deal with the problem that's been introduced with the inciting incident. In mythologist Joseph Campbell's terms, this is the "Refusal of the Call." The rest of Act Two focuses on the promise of the premise, or the scenes that show the hero either trying to solve the problem introduced or otherwise enjoying the moments of the inciting incident. We know it's the end of Act Two when the worst possible thing happens to our hero or he is farthest from solving the problem that was introduced at the end of Act One.

Act Three is abbreviated in a short film because it only involves the final wrap-up, so to speak. Typically, the hero solves the problem fairly quickly in this last act.

Let's consider the three-act structure of two very short films: *Black Hole,* which is based on the comic book by Charles Burns, and *Doodlebug* which is written and directed by Christopher Nolan. They're both under three minutes in length.

The first act of *Black Hole* sets up a sleep-deprived office worker who is in the copy room by himself late at night. The inciting incident occurs around forty-five seconds into the film when the hero discovers a black hole on a piece of copy paper. For some reason, he's able to put his hand through this hole and pick up his coffee cup. Act Two illustrates the "promise of the premise" as it revolves around the hero using the Black Hole to his advantage. This includes getting a free candy bar out of the vending machine as well as stacks of money from a locked safe. The midpoint comes when the hero notices the safe, eventually realizing that he can steal money. We see him tape the black hole onto the safe so he can grab stack after stack of cash out of the safe. Act Three shows the hero's greed, causing his ultimate downfall. His descent begins at 2:14 when the hero decides to steal from this safe. A further problem occurs when the black hole slips off the safe and our hero is trapped inside. The film ends with the protagonist knocking from the inside of the safe as the shots pull back, revealing the stark reality of the trapped worker.

Act One of *Doodlebug* sets up the story of a lone man in an apartment room, chasing something with his shoe in hand. The ominous music sets the tone of paranoia as we watch the man desperately trying to kill something, but he has no idea what it is. However we assume it's a bug of some sort. The use of black and white film as opposed to color gives the story a timeless feel. A minute into the film, the phone starts ringing. Act Two begins at 2:07 when it's revealed that the man is chasing a mini version of himself. Now the fun begins, hence "the promise of the premise." The man chases himself around with the shoe and ultimately catches himself. Act Two begins and ends when the man looks up and realizes there's a giant version of him lurking above, mimicking his actions. The larger version of the man is trying to kill the smaller man and so on. Suddenly, we hear a "Whack!" and the screen goes dark, signifying that our hero has been killed by his doppelganger. The third act in *Doodlebug* is incredibly short but it's nonetheless a definitive third act.

Beyond the obvious structural points in both *Black Hole* and *Doodlebug*, what makes these films resonate are their themes. When considering your structural beats, don't forget to include the all-important thematic element. In movies, themes reveal why you want to tell this story. What you're hoping to tell your audience and why you think it's so important. In *Black Hole*, the theme is crystal clear: greed is bad and will cause a person's downfall. In *Doodlebug*, the theme is more interpretative, but we believe the filmmaker wants to highlight the repetition of life and its never-ending loop. It's interesting to note that the filmmaker Christopher Nolan (*Doodlebug*) went on to explore this futility in life and the inability to make changes in his successful feature films, including *Inception* and *Interstellar*.

Now let's consider the structure of two slightly longer short films: The Dutch short film, *Gridlock* (seven minutes) by Dirk Belien and *The Lunch Date* (nine minutes) by Adam Davidson, which won the student Academy Award in 1991. Both short films have strong beginning, middle, and ends—or Acts One, Two, and Three, and can be viewed on YouTube. Spoiler alert! Please watch both these films before reading further.

In *The Lunch Date*, the movie opens with a rich white woman in her sixties walking casually through Grand Central Station in NYC after a successful day of shopping. We know all things about her because she wears a mink coat and carries several large shopping bags, including one from Bloomingdales. Everything is going fine when at exactly a minute into the film, a black man accidentally bumps into her, causing her to drop her purse and everything subsequently falls out.

The businessman attempts to help her with her things, but she refuses to let him. We get the sense that she's racist or at least afraid of black men. Because of this incident, she misses her train—an inciting incident. Now the second act commences as the woman now has to figure out what to do while waiting for a later train. She goes to the food court and buys a salad, then proceeds to wipe a table down—demonstrating that she's maybe not used to eating in a train terminal restaurant. She leaves her salad on the table to pick up a fork at the front of the restaurant, and when she walks back to her table, she's stunned to see a homeless black man sitting at her table and eating her salad. This occurs at exactly four minutes into the movie, marking it as the midpoint of the film. A dramatic shift occurs: the woman is no longer timid; she's a bit enraged. She tells the man it's her salad but he continues eating. And then, at five minutes, the woman actually starts to eat the salad with him. Watching a rich white woman sharing a salad with an apparently homeless black man is one of the great charms of this story, because we were shown that it's not what we should expect. Even the clerk at the counter is amazed. And when the black man gets two coffees for them, it further enhances the "promise of the premise." They enjoy each other's company, and it's a lovely scene. Act Two ends when the woman is back in the terminal and realizes she forgot her shopping bags in the restaurant. She then runs back, devastated to discover that not only is the man gone, but so are her bags. This occurs at 7:45 minutes into the film. Act Two endings are typically the worst possible thing for your protagonist. Act Three of *The Lunch Date* begins with some wonderful dramatic irony. The camera shows the woman's shopping bags in another booth, but she doesn't see them just yet. At that moment we know more than the character, which gives meaning to the audience—they're engaged. We know that she is at the wrong table and that the man didn't really take her bags. The moment when the she realizes her error, it's a priceless moment and a great zinger ending for the movie. We think and hope that her life will forever be altered by this man, and that she'll view black men differently. Of course, she does pass by a black man begging for money and doesn't give him anything. But perhaps that's because we've already established that she has no cash when she was struggling to purchase her salad. Thematically this is a rich movie about perception and it addresses the age-old saying, "Don't judge a book by its cover."

In *Gridlock*, an impatient businessman is stuck in traffic or a "gridlock." What's important in the opening scene is that the businessman is trying out his new cell phone for the first time and decides to call home to let his wife know that he's going to be late. On the other end of the phone, a little girl answers the phone. She's alone in a kitchen. She tells the impatient businessman, who we assume to be her father, that her mommy is upstairs with Uncle Vim. The businessman looks startled and is clearly wondering who "Uncle Vim" is. Act Two is all about discovering who Uncle Vim is and the realization that the man's wife is cheating on him. Act Two ends with the two graphic deaths of the wife and Uncle Vim, one dying by falling in a swimming pool. Death is usually a low point in any story. Act Three is rapid-paced, but it packs a powerful punch as we learn that the businessman doesn't have a swimming pool. We quickly realize that he's not even talking to his own daughter and therefore his wife wasn't cheating with someone named Uncle Vim. Thematically, this movie isn't as strong as *Lunch Date,* but it's a good cautionary tale for dialing the wrong phone number.

WORLD BUILDING

Before you begin writing your script, you have to know the *world*. In this context, world refers to more than just the geography. True, it can mean the world of Africa or some other foreign country, the world of New York City, or the world of a doctor's office. Or maybe it's not a physical place but a fantasy world. Once you know the world, you need to personalize it by being very specific. So if it's the world of New York City, where in New York City? Maybe it's midtown in the theatre district and to further specify it, it's the world of a large Broadway show like *Wicked*. Or it's the world of Off-Broadway with a very small show. Even though every movie has certain constants, such as three acts, they become less clichéd when you build a specific world.

In terms of structure, you need to set up the world of the story early in the structure. Let's consider the worlds for recent TV shows and films:

Blackish, a network comedy, takes place in Los Angeles, but it exists in the world where an upwardly mobile black family lives in an affluent white neighborhood where they are the only black family. The mother is a doctor and the husband is an advertising executive. Their four children attend private schools, and their relatives from the "hood of South Central" make fun of them for being too "white." The world is integral to the humor in the sitcom.

Orphan Black, a cable sci-fi show, takes place in a world where cloning exists—and not just with one or two clones, but an unknown number of clones of the same woman. That's what makes the show so great.

Jessica Jones, a Marvel series on Netflix, takes place in Hell's Kitchen in New York City, but the world is one where superheroes live anonymously side-by-side with their peers and the titular character has enormous strength even though she's slight in stature.

The Green Room, an indie thriller film, takes place in the world of skinheads, which are neo-Nazis and drug dealers, but we don't know all of that at first. In the beginning, we think we're just at a punk concert, and the world is revealed slowly.

No Country for Old Men, winner of the Academy Award for Best Adapted Screenplay in 2008, takes place in the remote Texas desert near the Mexican border. A sheriff's voice-over opens the film with desert shots onscreen. We don't even meet the sheriff until thirty minutes into the movie. By then the world is fully established as a dangerous place where drugs, money, and murder are prevalent. At its core, the story is about a murderous villain, but what makes it special is the world.

Little Miss Sunshine, winner of the Academy Award for Best Original Screenplay in 2010, is built on the world of a dysfunctional family living in Albuquerque, New Mexico. In quick succession, we meet all the family members and are introduced to their quirks. Their level of dysfunction is what makes this story so unique.

Open Endings

In the structure of short film, the opening is paramount because it pulls us into the story. Our enjoyment continues in the second act as we watch our hero making the most of the premise that was established in the first act. But in a short film, perhaps most important of all is that quixotic, thrilling ending, where we are treated to a zinger story point that completely takes us by surprise. From the ending of *Black Hole* when the man is stuck in a safe, to *Gridlock* when the man realizes he dialed the wrong number, to *Lunch Date* when the lady realizes she was at the wrong table—all of these stories have "open endings" because we don't know what happens next for our character. But that's okay, because the ending of the short film made us think about the message that's being communicated through its story. In *Black Hole*, we've been made to realize that greed is bad. In *Lunch Date*, we've realized that we can't judge people based on how they look.

Now let's consider the short film *Consent* by Jason Reitman, who later went on to make *Juno* and other feature films. In the first act of *Consent*, we meet two college students (a male and a female) making out in a dorm room. The girl stops and tells the boy they should pause. The boy agrees that he should get something—where the audience assumes he's going to get a condom. The inciting incident then occurs as the girl's male lawyer suddenly appears in the room with them, holding up a legal document. Then the boy's female lawyer pops into the room. Now the movie is going in a new direction and we've established that these two lawyers arguing over documents will determine what sexual acts their clients will and won't participate in.

In the second act, the story focuses on the promise of the premise. Instead of saying "blow job" or "oral sex," the dialogue refers to sexual acts as item numbers in a legal document. The act concludes with the lawyers settling on an agreement. Note that this isn't the worst case scenario for our protagonists, but it is a clear act break. There are times where the second act break is not the lowest point, but rather a turning point to something new. In the third act of *Consent*, the young lovers start making out again when the door opens. The girl's roommate walks in, and suddenly, looks interested. She asks if she should bring in her lawyer—implying that she's thinking about a threesome. And the movie finds its resolution with an open ending: *Will there be a threesome?*

While we can argue that there is a specific structure for a short film, writers should take note that if structure gets in the way of a really good story, it should be altered. We don't want you to think that writing a script is like painting by numbers.

Writer/Director James Schamus (The Ice Storm, Crouching Tiger, Hidden Dragon) was recently quoted saying, "When you have finished a screenplay, you have created approximately 124 pages of begging for money and attention" ("History of Screenwriting," *Script Lab)*. Screenplays have to do double-duty as both an art form and a blueprint for the physical act of film production. Understanding structure enables you to accomplish both the art and the practicality of telling a story for the screen.

ENDNOTES

1. http://blog.nationalmediamuseum.org.uk/louis-le-prince-created-the-first-ever-moving-pictures/

2. https://en.wikipedia.org/wiki/Poetics_(Aristotle)

3. https://www.screentakes.com/an-evolutionary-study-of-the-three-act-structure-model-in-drama/

4. https://archive.org/stream/freytagstechniqu00freyuoft/freytagstechniqu00freyuoft_djvu.txt

5. https://www.screentakes.com/an-evolutionary-study-of-the-three-act-structure-model-in-drama/

SHORT FILM STRUCTURE

One way to really understand how film structure works is to reverse-engineer a short film. We'll start by doing this in the broadest terms. We won't get into too much detail.

List the major story beats of the movie. You will have about 20 story beats.

Identify which story beats belong to the:

FIRST ACT   SECOND ACT

MID-POINT   THIRD ACT

USE THE WORKSHEET ON THE NEXT PAGE
TO IDENTIFY THE BEATS IN YOUR STORY.

LIST YOUR TV SHOW OR MOVIE: _____

ACT ONE

_____
_____
_____

STORY BEAT

_____
_____
_____
_____
_____
_____
_____

ACT TWO

_____
_____
_____

_____
_____
_____
_____
_____

MID-POINT

_____
_____
_____

_____
_____
_____
_____
_____
_____
_____

ACT THREE

_____
_____
_____

_____
_____
_____
_____

CHAPTER 7

What to Write, Why to Write?

NEVER CHASE THE WAVE

We once asked a student why she was taking our class. She said her hope was to learn how to write a full-length screenplay, sell it, and then pay off her student loans. That was not a good reason.

As a writer, a common question you'll be asked is: "What are you working on?" This is the part where you might give a "logline"—the one-line description of the script you're writing. But the real writer knows the question should be not *what* to write, but *why* you're writing.

You should not write anything for the purpose of selling it. You should write scripts because you have a need and a desire to say something about the human condition. You want to share a great story.

The young writer who hates horror should not write a horror movie, because horror movies are selling. The writer should never chase the wave.

Every time a movie makes money, it inspires a feeding frenzy among the sharks (agents and executives alike) looking to feed on similar scripts. After *Crocodile Dundee* came out, the question around town was: "Can you set it in Australia?" They didn't even care about the subject—they were chasing the wave from down under. When zombies got hot, there were a lot of zombies.

The *Die Hard* formula had been pitched so much that it finally died when someone pitched *Die Hard* in a building. The wave finally crashed.

Warner Brothers is chasing the Marvel wave. Marvel has done an amazing job balancing story and spectacle on the big screen as well as putting their content on television (Netflix). Warner Brothers seems to be trying to catch the wave, but instead has been drowning in mediocrity.

No one knows when that wave will crash down. In the first wave of superhero movies in the early 2000s, a charming script, *My Super Ex-Girlfriend*, became a so-so movie. For whatever reasons, it did not work as well at the box office as the studios had hoped. Suddenly, anything with the word "super" in it was dead property.

Hollywood will use the wave of success to tell you what they think they want.

Hollywood will use the wave of failure to tell you what they don't want. They have a hard time seeing two years into the future when that wave is long gone. So how does a writer survive in this tsunami of indecisiveness?

A writer must be writing the movie that they want to see and making a splash with their original material.

Hollywood will always chase the wave of money that is flowing into another movie company's box office, but that doesn't mean the writer should chase the wave. The writer *is* the wave: the force and the emotion. Swim in the ocean that you get to name.

You might be thinking that all the studios seem to make is superhero movies. The box office has changed. Let's look back at 1982 and the top ten movies at that time:

- ▶ *E.T. The Extra-Terrestrial*—original screenplay
- ▶ *Tootsie*—original screenplay
- ▶ *An Officer and a Gentleman*—original screenplay
- ▶ *Rocky III*—sequel; third in a series
- ▶ *Porky's*—original screenplay
- ▶ *Star Trek II: The Wrath of Kahn*—sequel
- ▶ *48 Hours*—original screenplay
- ▶ *Poltergeist*—original screenplay
- ▶ *The Best Little Whorehouse in Texas*—based on a musical
- ▶ *Annie*—based on a musical

Out of these ten screenplays, comedy, action, drama, science fiction, broad comedy, and musical are the genres. And six of the movies are original screenplays.

Let's jump to ten years later to 1992:

- ▶ *Aladdin*—original screenplay
- ▶ *Home Alone 2: Lost in New York*—sequel
- ▶ *Batman Returns*—sequel
- ▶ *Lethal Weapon 3*—sequel
- ▶ *A Few Good Men*—based on pre-existing material
- ▶ *Sister Act*—original screenplay
- ▶ *The Bodyguard*—original screenplay
- ▶ *Wayne's World*—based on pre-existing material
- ▶ *Basic Instinct*—original screenplay
- ▶ *A League of Their Own*—original screenplay

Ten years later and original screenplays are still holding their own with five out of ten. Two of the films are based on pre-existing materials (a play and an SNL sketch), but now there are three sequels.

Let's jump ten more years to 2002—things start to change a little.

- *Spider-Man*—based on pre-existing material
- *The Lord of the Rings: The Two Towers*—sequel; based on pre-existing material
- *Stars Wars: Episode II—Attack of the Clones*—sequel; based on pre-existing material
- *Harry Potter and the Chamber of Secrets*—sequel; based on pre-existing material
- *My Big Fat Greek Wedding*—original screenplay
- *Signs*—original screenplay
- *Austin Powers in Goldmember*—sequel
- *Men in Black II*—sequel
- *Ice Age*—original; animated
- *Chicago*—based on a musical

There are now only three original screenplays. Audiences are at home watching the new golden age of television. When they do go to the movies, it's for the spectacle. Something big.

We jump now to 2012, where the top movies were:

- *Marvel's The Avengers*—sequel; based on pre-existing material
- *The Dark Knight Rises*—sequel; based on pre-existing material
- *The Hunger Games*—based on pre-existing material
- *The Amazing Spider-Man*—a reboot; based on pre-existing material
- *Brave*—original; animation
- *Ted*—original screenplay
- *Madagascar 3: Europe's Most Wanted*—sequel; based on pre-existing material
- *Dr. Seuss' Lorax*—based on pre-existing material
- *MIB 3*—sequel; based on pre-existing material
- *Ice Age: Continental Drift*—sequel; based on pre-existing material

There are only two original screenplays in the top ten, and one features a foul-mouthed talking bear.

Hollywood has always adapted from novels, and there was a time when TV shows were rebooted as movies (*Charlie's Angels*, *The Brady Bunch*). Now, old movies are rebooted as TV shows (*Lethal Weapon*, *Teen Wolf*) and TV shows are being remade as new TV shows (*Battlestar Galactica*, *The Odd Couple*). Hollywood loves material that they believe has a following or a possible audience waiting to watch a new TV show or movie. The acclaimed TV show *Homeland* is based on the Israeli show *Prisoners of War*.

Other forces can influence content. DVD sales plummeted when in-home streaming arrived, and Hollywood now recognizes that American audiences are only 10 percent of the movie-viewing audience. Because of this, the studios started making bigger movies with more spectacles that translate well to any audience.

Well, you might be asking yourself: "Since they're selling right now, shouldn't I be writing a great big idea?" No. We said the writer should not be chasing the wave, but that doesn't mean they shouldn't be aware of the trends in Hollywood.

We believe that if the screenwriter can pull off a low budget, character-based story, the path is easier to the top in Hollywood. If you write something true and moving or create a character that people can't stop talking about, there is a chance you will be in demand.

Christopher Nolan went from *Doodlebug,* to *Following,* to *Memento,* Batman and the world of Gotham, to outer space, and finally, he's currently filming his World War II movie.

Damien Chazelle's career traveled through *Guy and Madeline on a Park Bench* (his film school thesis film) to *Whiplash* (the short and then the feature) to the big studio film *La-La Land.* The studios didn't know they were making original musicals until *La-La Land* landed on their desk and they wanted to be in business with Damien Chazelle.

DEVELOPING LOGLINES

The studios and networks always love the concepts that are "uniquely familiar" to them. These are projects whose loglines sound like they could be films or shows, but never have.

What's a logline you might ask? A logline is a one-line description of the movie or short film or television show. It's not a long, complicated pitch. Instead, it presents the basics of the story in one sentence, sometimes two. It doesn't dive deep into the character but hints at character and doesn't tell you the whole story but sets up the story.

Breaking Bad is a drama about a high school science teacher dying from cancer who begins making and selling crystal meth.

Divorce is a comedy about a middle-aged woman and her husband going through a long, drawn-out divorce.

Iron Man equates to: after being held captive in an Afghan cave, billionaire engineer Tony Stark creates a unique weaponized suit of armor to fight evil.

A logline suggests the movie; it's like looking at a web-site or a movie guide and seeing what a movie is about. You don't want to know the whole story, you just want to know if it's worth seeing or if you're even interested.

You want to make us want to see the movie.

Feature Film Loglines

Feature film loglines differ from short film loglines. Let's look at some feature film loglines of screenplays that made the famous "blacklist" of the current best screenplays in Hollywood.

Stronger
   by John Pollono, Scott Silver
   The true story of Jeff Bauman, who after losing his legs in the 2013 Boston Marathon bombing, was an integral part of helping police locate the suspects.

The Libertine
> by Ben Kopit
> After the Head of the French National Assembly is placed under house arrest for accusations of sexual assault, he must live in a guarded apartment with his estranged wife until the case comes to a close.

Rocket
> by Jeffrey Gelber, Ryan Belenzon
> Roger "The Rocket" Clemens, one of the greatest pitchers of all time, has 4,672 strikeouts, 354 wins, and a record 7 Cy Young awards. This is the story of why he is not in the Hall of Fame.

Crater
> by John J. Griffin
> On the moon, five teens take an unauthorized and adventure-filled road trip, just before one of them is to be sent away on a seventy-five year journey to another planet, leaving behind his best friends.

Miss Sloane
> by Jonathan "Jonny" Perera
> A powerful lobbyist sacrifices her career on Capitol Hill so she can push through an amendment enforcing stricter federal laws regulating guns.

True Fan
> by John Whittington
> After interfering with a foul ball during a Chicago Cubs playoff game, Steve Bartman was tortured and stalked by die-hard Cub fans for potentially costing them their first National League pennant since 1945. Years later, in a new town with a new identity—but depressed, overweight, and working a dead-end job—Steve meets a woman who gives him a new lease on life and reason to live.

Please note that the "best" scripts were all about character. Yes, one was on the moon but there was not a dragon in sight. We love *Game of Thrones*, but David Benioff wrote *The 25th Hour* which led to *Troy*, which lead to *Game of Thrones*.

The above loglines all suggest long and large battles about gun legislation, steroid trials, and a road trip on the moon. They all seem great and all suggest many events unfolding in their 120 minutes of screen-time.

We sometimes see a student attempt to jam a two-hour film into ten to fifteen pages. The problem is this: movies and television shows are about many events. Short films usually revolve around one main event. Here are some loglines from the world-renowned Sundance Film Festival.

Short Film Loglines (examples)

Affections

Written and directed by Bridey Elliott. U.S.A., sixteen minutes

This comedy about isolation and loneliness follows a young woman who is adrift and seeking intimacy in the most unlikely places.

Bacon & God's Wrath

Written and directed by Sol Friedman. Canada, nine minutes

A ninety-year-old Jewish woman reflects on her life experiences as she prepares to try bacon for the first time.

Edmond

Written and directed by Nina Gantz. United Kingdom, nine minutes

Edmond's impulse to love and be close to others is strong—maybe too strong. As he stands by a lake contemplating his options, he reflects on his defining moments in search of the origin of his desires.

Her Friend Adam

Written and directed by Ben Petrie. Canada, seventeen minutes

A boyfriend's jealous impulse spirals out of control in sixteen minutes of romantic doom.

Jungle

Written and directed by Asantewaa Prempeh. U.S.A., thirteen minutes

The lines between trust, betrayal, and forgiveness are intertwined for two Senegalese vendors as they try to make a living on the streets of New York City.

The Grandfather Drum

Written and directed by Michelle Derosier. Canada, thirteen minutes

As the balance of the world turns upside down for the Anishinabek people, the elder Naamowin builds a healing drum to save his grandson and his people.

The Procedure

Written and directed by Calvin Lee Reeder. U.S.A., four minutes

A man is captured and forced to endure a strange experiment.

Thunder Road

Written and directed by Jim Cummings. U.S.A., thirteen minutes

Officer Arnaud loved his mom.

The last logline is too brief, but the film is wonderful. A comedic and sad film, it's about a police officer, Arnaud, who says a few words at his mother's funeral; those few words are him singing Bruce Springsteen's classic *Thunder Road.*

Go back and look at the short film loglines. The story is centered about one event. This usually takes place in a compressed about of time. Where features take place from ninety minutes to over two hours, short films range from four to seventeen minutes in the listing above.

Did you notice anything else?

"Written and directed" appear in all of the above shorts. You can write your way into Hollywood, but you can film your way in faster. Write your script *and* direct it!

Here are a few more logline examples.

International Narrative Shorts

Baby / United Kingdom (Director and Screenwriter: Daniel Mulloy)
> A young woman intervenes when she witnesses men mugging a girl. Now they won't leave her alone.

BLOKES / Chile (Director: Marialy Rivas)
> Thirteen-year-old Luchito fantasizes about Manuel, his sixteen-year-old neighbor, whom he can see standing by a window in an adjacent project building. Oblivious of the gaze of his precocious voyeur, Manuel discovers his own sexuality with a girl from the neighborhood.

Cinderella / Brazil, France (Director and Screenwriter: Magali Magistry)
> Luiza and Rico. Love and loss in a Rio nightclub.

Deeper Than Yesterday / Australia (Director and Screenwriter: Ariel Kleiman)
> After three months submerged underwater in a submarine, the crew have become savages. Oleg, one of the men onboard, fears that losing perspective may mean losing himself.

Diarchy / Italy (Director and Screenwriter: Ferdinando Cito Filmomarino)
> Giano and Luc are traveling through the woods when a storm breaks, forcing them to take shelter in Luc's villa. Gradually and insidiously, a competition emerges between them, with terrible consequences.

The Legend of Beaver Dam / Canada (Director: Jerome Sable; Screenwriters: Jerome Sable and Eli Batalion)
> When a ghost story around the campfire awakens an evil monster, it's up to nerdy Danny Zigwitz to be the hero and save his fellow campers from a bloody massacre.

Little Brother / United Kingdom (Director: Callum Cooper; Screenwriters: Callum Cooper in collaboration with Oni Family)

A teenage boy uses his hearing impairment to escape his daily routine and the responsibility of looking after his wheelchair-bound little brother.

Love Birds / Czech Republic (Director and Screenwriter: Brian Lye)

A humorous love story that reflects the similarities between bird and human life.

Shikasha / Japan (Director and Screenwriter: Isamu Hirabayashi)

Imprisoned and bound, a mother and child lay in darkness as investigators search a wasteland.

Small Change / Ireland (Director and Screenwriter: Cathy Brady)

Karen, a young single mother, is bored by routine as slot machines have become her secret thrill and addiction. With Christmas looming, a desperate hope for a big win sees her life spiral out of control.

SPRING / United Kingdom (Director and Screenwriter: Hong Khaou)

A young man meets a stranger for an experience that will change his life forever.

Stopover / Italy, Romania (Director: Ioana Uricau; Screenwriter: Cristian Mungiu)

Lost and found in-between plane rides.

The Wind is Blowing on My Street / Iran, USA (Director and Screenwriter: Saba Riazi)

A young girl in Tehran accidentally gets left on the street with no head scarf. She is forced to interact with a neighbor who keeps her company in an environment where her mishap could equal trouble.

Even internationally the structure of the short film remains the same focusing its narrative around one key event.

DEVELOPING THE SHORT FILM

The winner of the Student Academy Award for Short Film went to *Day One*, a twenty-five minute film set in Afghanistan. The drama focuses on an Afghan interpreter for the U.S. Army who is forced to deliver the child of an enemy bomb-maker. The same rules of drama apply to short film; the difference is in the structure.

So, where you do start? We recommend that you start with the "world" of your story. You, as a writer, should explore that world; to figure out the story before writing the story. The first step is to just make a list of everything that you can possibly think of that is associated with the world of your story.

IMAGES—what do you see? How does the world look? Is it fun and warm? Dark and gritty?

LOCATIONS—if you are not thinking about directing your own short (which we hope you are), what locations do you have access to? Limited locations can sometimes be a blessing; it forces you to focus on characters. In the short film, *God of Love,* the locations are a club, an apartment, and some outdoor New York footage.

CHARACTERS—who is the main character in your story and what are they doing? Remember that *action is character.* Here's an example of the logline of the film *Small Change:* Karen, a young single mother is bored by routine as slot machines have become her secret thrill and addiction. With Christmas looming, a desperate hope for a big win sees her life spiral out of control. Her action is the gambling.

Write your logline. Test it on friends. Are they confused? Do they see the movie when they read the logline? When you are first developing ideas, your pitch or logline might be met with silence. This isn't a good sign—but when people react and want to contribute ideas, that is a great sign.

Three-Sentence Summary

You have the idea, now it is time to start working on fleshing it out. Write the entire short film in three sentences: A beginning, middle, and end. Once again, test it out. As discussed in the "Structure" chapter, not every film has to have a closed ending. Open endings are sometimes as good, if not better, in the short film. You want to leave the audience reacting.

The Main Character

Write a backstory for your main character. Who is the protagonist? What are their traits? What is their belief system? How do they look physically? How do they act? The more you know, the more you can show. You want to know your main character as well as you can so things like an art poster or world map poster that hangs in their room has meaning and might pay off later in the script.

Expand the Three Sentences into a Page

You now want to show us you are a storyteller. Take that protagonist and the short version of the script and write a one-page summary of the short film. What are we seeing? Write it as it unfolds.

Share with friends, or better yet, share this with other writers. Some will like it, and some won't know what to say—but you know how to take notes. You want to keep reworking the idea and the script.

The Importance of the Logline

No, this is not in the wrong spot. We wanted to circle back to the logline. As Monroe Star says in *The Last Tycoon*, "Just because it [the script] is better does not mean it's good." You can write a great script but the logline and story have to work before you can write the whole thing.

As you develop your short film, watch as many short films as you can. They are on many websites like Short of the Week, and you can find hundreds of shorts on YouTube. You can buy the Oscar-Nominated Shorts on Amazon or iTunes.

The more you watch, the more you will learn and realize it takes a long time to write a short film.

LOGLINES

Ideas can come to us as we're waking up or when we're running through a park or driving to work. But what if you had to generate an idea on the spot? What if you didn't have the luxury of waiting for that idea to pop into your head?

Here's an exercise that will force you to come up with ideas.

1 Sit down with a magazine. Look at the cover and in the space at the bottom of this page, write down one or two words that come to mind when you look at the cover image.

2 Turn the page and repeat.

3 By the end of the 2–3 minute scene, you should have about 5–7 beats.

4 Don't censor yourself. Ignore the voice in your head telling you it's not worth writing down. Just list the word that immediately pops into your head.

5 By the end, you should have a list of at least 20 words. Take some of the words and write them into loglines. These loglines can become the idea for a short film.

USE THE WORKSHEET ON THE NEXT PAGE TO TRY THIS EXERCISE.

logline exercise

LIST THE WORDS HERE:

_____ _____ _____ _____

_____ _____ _____ _____

_____ _____ _____ _____

_____ _____ _____ _____

_____ _____ _____ _____

NOW WRITE TWO POSSIBLE LOGLINES BASED ON THE WORDS ABOVE:

1 _____

_____

2 _____

_____

LOGLINES
(CONTINUED)

This is an exercise a manager once had us do to generate ideas for loglines.

For example, here is the logline for *The Searchers*. A Civil War veteran embarks on a journey to rescue his niece from an Indian tribe. It's a western.

Let's change it to a horror film. And update it to present day.

The protagonist was a civil war veteran played by John Wayne.

We're going to go with a female Iraq vet whose 18-year-old niece is kidnapped by a vampire king. Instead of the old west, we're on the brink of the apocalypse. Our hero has to search all of hell to save her niece before she is married off to Satan. The title: *HELL ON EARTH*. Here's another example:

Choose an existing TV Show or Movie	"Easy Rider"—Drama/road movie about two counter-culture hippies who drive drugs to New Orleans.
Change the Genre	Drama road movie to Science Fiction
Change the Protagonist	Hard-edged female biker agrees to transport stolen D.N.A. across the badlands of future Mad Max–like America.
Give it a New Title	D.N.A.
Write the Logline for the New Show	VIV, a hard-edged female biker agrees to transport stolen D.N.A. across the badlands of future Mad Max–like America.

USE THE WORKSHEET ON THE NEXT PAGE
TO TRY THIS EXERCISE.

logline exercise #2

Okay, now it's your turn. In 30 minutes, come up with 10 new ideas.

**Choose an existing
TV Show or Movie**

Change the Genre

**Change
the Protagonist**

Give it a New Title

**Write the Logline for
the New Show**

**Choose an existing
TV Show or Movie**

Change the Genre

**Change
the Protagonist**

Give it a New Title

**Write the Logline for
the New Show**

logline exercise #2

Choose an existing
TV Show or Movie

Change the Genre

Change
the Protagonist

Give it a New Title

Write the Logline for
the New Show

Choose an existing
TV Show or Movie

Change the Genre

Change
the Protagonist

Give it a New Title

Write the Logline for
the New Show

logline exercise #2

Choose an existing
TV Show or Movie

Change the Genre

Change
the Protagonist

Give it a New Title

Write the Logline for
the New Show

Choose an existing
TV Show or Movie

Change the Genre

Change
the Protagonist

Give it a New Title

Write the Logline for
the New Show

logline exercise #2

Choose an existing
TV Show or Movie

Change the Genre

Change
the Protagonist

Give it a New Title

Write the Logline for
the New Show

Choose an existing
TV Show or Movie

Change the Genre

Change
the Protagonist

Give it a New Title

Write the Logline for
the New Show

logline exercise #2

Choose an existing
TV Show or Movie

Change the Genre

Change
the Protagonist

Give it a New Title

Write the Logline for
the New Show

Choose an existing
TV Show or Movie

Change the Genre

Change
the Protagonist

Give it a New Title

Write the Logline for
the New Show

logline exercise #2

Choose an existing
TV Show or Movie

Change the Genre

Change
the Protagonist

Give it a New Title

Write the Logline for
the New Show

Choose an existing
TV Show or Movie

Change the Genre

Change
the Protagonist

Give it a New Title

Write the Logline for
the New Show

Look them over now. Do they have any promise?
We bet they do.

logline exercise #3

WATCH 3 SHORT FILMS.

WRITE THE LOGLINES FOR EACH FILM.

1

2

3

CHAPTER 8

Developing the Short Screenplay

If you've been doing the exercises for each chapter, we've had you working on very short scripts of no more than five pages, and we've put you in a straitjacket by telling you to write only visuals or dialogue, and we've given you a prompt that gives you the genesis of a plot that involves conflict. Now it's time to spread your wings and write a ten- to fifteen-page script entirely on your own. Here's a step-by-step process to develop that script, and more than anything else, you need to know that you must break down the story thoroughly before you begin writing. The last thing you want to do is turn on your computer and begin typing on an empty page; the blank page is your nemesis. Breaking the story is as important as actually writing the story. Professional screenwriters spend months and months breaking a feature script before they begin to write. We hope you will spend at least a few days developing your short script before starting to write.

BREAKING THE STORY

There are many ways to "break" the story. But remember: story is there for characters to change. Start by thinking about characters that interest you. This could be an arrogant barista who served you your latte this morning. Or a shy classmate who couldn't look you in the eye. Then put them in conflict in a situation that will force them to change. The barista spills hot coffee and is fired. Now he has to find a new job. And the trouble is he's not good at anything but making and serving coffee. Now he starts to get humble. Or consider the shy classmate who returns to her dorm and her roommate has turned into a witch and is chanting in front of an open cauldron. Our shy co-ed will have to find her voice to solve this dilemma. So once you've established a problem for your character, the plot will begin to emerge. Take a moment and think of some possible ideas for your film.

The Logline

Carve that idea into a logline. Remember that this should be one sentence. Mention your character and the problem that's thrown at them, then pitch your logline to everyone who will listen including your roommates, partners, teachers, or even the barista. The point is to notice how people react. If their eyes light up, you're onto something. If they look confused, or worse, bored, ask them why. After this, try refining your logline until it creates excitement in your listener. Write in your logline here:

_____

_____

_____

_____

Major Plot Points

Figure out the big, major beats in your story, then make a list of these on white index cards. You should know your characters, world, inciting incident, midpoint, end of Act Two and, yes, the ending of your movie.

Screenwriting is not a genre where you figure it out as you type. There will be plenty of time for other kinds of discovery as you write, but the ending is not something that you figure out when you're on the last page.

SPEED PITCHING

The next tool we like to use in breaking a story is speed pitching. This is when you pitch your story idea multiple times in a one-on-one environment in rapid succession. It's kind of like speed dating in that you get to talk to a lot of people in a very short period of time. Unlike speed dating, you don't need to worry about meeting Mr. or Ms. Right. You do, however, need to tell an encapsulated version of your story over and over. It may sound tiring, and it can be, but it's also uplifting when you pitch your story beats multiple times and you begin to hear what really works about your idea. You also need to be open to feedback from each person you meet. Now, if you hear a specific critique from someone and you don't agree with it, then don't bother incorporating that note into your story. However, if you get the same note multiple times, we urge you to consider making a change to your story—even if you might not initially agree with it. The real purpose of speed pitching is not so you can hear yourself talk, but so you can figure out how to improve your story before you begin writing it.

We've tried speed pitching in a variety of intervals, from three to seven minutes long. What we've found is that the five-minute speed pitch works really well. First we'll address the logistics of setting up a speed pitch and then we'll discuss what aspects of your story you should include.

The Speed Pitch Logistics

This works in a classroom. It also works with a writers group. If you are the only one of your friends working on a script, tell each friend the story and ask for feedback. Gather at least ten people, and then create two lines and have everyone face someone else. Make yourself responsible for the time clock. Announce that it's time for the speed pitch to begin and set the timer for five minutes. Have all the people on one side pitch their story idea to the person across from them. Ideally, they'll finish pitching their story in about three minutes so that it gives the listener two minutes to give some feedback. Once those five minutes are up, stop everyone and have one row step to the right. The person at the end will walk down to the other end. Continue on this way until everyone has pitched their story to five people. By the end of this twenty-five minute period, everyone will have a better sense of what works and what doesn't in their short film idea. We've also tried this with participants sitting down at desks. This can be good because the person getting feedback on their pitch can more easily write down the notes. We've also tried this in a circle with a larger group of fifteen to twenty students. But we've come to the conclusion that speed pitching works best when people are standing up because there's more energy and excitement.

What to Include in Your Speed Pitch

To begin, get yourself ten blank index cards. The goal is to not overwrite here, but to keep it simple. You'll need to tell your story in about three minutes, so if you put too much information on your cards, the story will get bogged down and your listener will become bored and be unable to give any feedback. On one side of the index card, write the word listed below in all capital letters. Then on the other side, explain that particular beat.

CARD #1: LOGLINE—Write down the logline. This is easy because you've already worked hard on it.

CARD #2: WORLD—Describe the place and situation in which your main character is living when the story begins. This is the status quo for your hero, or rather, what their life is like if the movie never happens. It's important to establish this before you begin your story.

CARD #3: CHARACTERS—Describe your protagonist in terms of age, sex, name, occupation, and outlook on life. Then briefly describe any other important characters.

CARD #4: HOOK—Describe what's happening in the first scene in your movie—the one that grabs your viewer or reader and makes them want to continue watching or reading.

CARD #5: INCITING INCIDENT—Explain what happens to turn the plot in a new direction. This is the problem for the character, and up until this point, the character is living in their world.

CARD #6: SECOND ACT SCENES—Talk about three possible scenes that will illustrate the "promise of your premise." So if you have a comedy, describe three funny scenes—similarly, if it's a drama, three serious scenes, and three scary scenes for a horror film. The scenes will reflect your genre. Does each scene push the story forward?

CARD #7: MIDPOINT—Describe the halfway point of the movie. It's another major plot point that turns the movie in a new direction, and it's also typically when your protagonist really starts to change.

CARD #8: END OF SECOND ACT—Describe the darkest moment for the hero—the farthest from solving their problem. However, they might also suddenly have a new goal.

CARD #9: ENDING OF MOVIE—Tell us the resolution of the story. A zinger ending works best for a short film, like a surprise twist to your story. Something we never expected.

CARD #10: THEME—On the back of this card, tell us why you are writing this movie or why this story is so important to you or your characters. You need to have something to say if you're going to write a script. A message to impart.

What's Next?

Once speed pitching is over, take everything you've written on those cards and the notes you received from your listeners and type it into your screenplay program. This will be the beginning of your beat sheet that will then become your scriptment.

BEAT SHEET

The beat sheet is a list of everything that happens in your movie, specifically the cause and effects in the story. You can make your beat sheet as detailed as you like but here are the sixteen beats that we feel are most important to include when writing a short film. To aid us in understanding these beats, let's first watch two award-winning short films, *Miracle Fish* and *I Love Sarah Jane*. Both films can be found for free on YouTube. Once you've watched these films, consider the following:

Beats in the Structure of a Short Film

FIRST ACT BEATS

(1) OPENING HOOK

Just like in a feature film, this is that moment when you grab your audience. Sometimes it's an exciting event like an opening action scene in any Marvel movie. Other times it's a gathering for a birthday or a funeral or a graduation. Other times it's a chance to shock us. Consider the opening of *I Love Sarah Jane*. It begins with Jimbo, a thirteen-year-old boy who is riding his bike. But it's not just any bike ride through suburbia, he's riding his bike through what looks like a war zone. Smoke plumes in the background, he carries a bow and arrows on his bike, and no one seems to be around until we notice there's blood on the mailbox and dead bodies on the ground. That all happens in the very first minute. Does it grab our attention? You bet it does! That's what you want with your opening hook.

(2) DEFINING ACTION—INTRODUCE CHARACTERS

A defining action is what the characters are doing when we first see them. What a person does says more about them than their dialogue. Or, again, as Aristotle said, "Action defines character." By introducing our characters doing something specific and interesting, we draw the reader into the world and quickly establish the tone. In *Miracle Fish*, the movie opens with an eight-year-old boy saying goodbye to his mother at the entrance to his school. From the very first scene, our attention is piqued because we learn that it's the boy's birthday and his father is in the hospital. We also sense that something is slightly peculiar with the boy. He seems to be alone everywhere: he sits in class alone, and at lunch he's by himself except for two boys who make fun of him for his lame fish toy that he got as a birthday gift. In *I Love Sarah Jane*, the boy has a photo of Sarah Jane taped to his bike. It's clear that he's interested in her. He doesn't care he has to ride through zombie carnage and deal with a teen gang of boys to see her.

(3) EXPOSITION

This beat establishes the who, what, where, and when of the movie. These are the details that fill in your character's world. In *Miracle Fish*, we see that the boy is a loner and he goes to an elementary school where he has no friends. At the end of lunch, he decides not to return to class and slips into the nurse's office unnoticed, establishing that he's someone who can slip through the cracks. In *I Love Sarah Jane*, the boy rides his bike to a house where other boys are hanging out. But instead of playing a ball game, they fire arrows at zombies.

(4) SOMETHING HAPPENS—THE INCITING INCIDENT

This beat is the end of the first act. It's when something disrupts the protagonist's routine and kicks the story into gear. In a short film, this beat typically happens about a quarter of the way through a movie in terms of screen time. In *Miracle Fish*, this moment is when the boy wakes up alone in the nurse's office and steps into the hallway, but there is no one to be found. Now he has a problem: Where is everyone? What's happened? In *I Love Sarah Jane*, the boy leaves the other guys to go into the house to find Sarah Jane. At four minutes into the film, the boy finds Sarah Jane. But she's not thrilled to see him, so now he has to win the love of Sarah Jane.

SECOND ACT BEATS

(5) CONFLICT

The second act begins by showing the hero trying to solve the problem that was just introduced. In *Miracle Fish*, the boy is completely alone and he has to figure out where everyone is. We see him riding a skateboard through the hall and drawing on the chalkboard, and at this point we're laughing with him as he enjoys the moments of being alone at school, having the freedom to do as he pleases. In *I Love Sarah Jane*, we watch as Jimbo awkwardly tries to talk to Sarah Jane, and without much success.

(6) MIDDLE OF YOUR STORY

In a short film, there are an undefined number of scenes that show our protagonist trying to solve their problems. In *Miracle Fish*, we see the boy looking around an empty classroom where it's obvious that the students have left in a hurry. He notices a book about aliens and that prompts us to wonder if perhaps an alien abduction has caused all the students to suddenly disappear. In *I Love Sarah Jane*, our character ignores the boys and moves to the couch to sit with Sarah Jane.

(7) REVEAL CHARACTER INSIGHT

When the protagonist is trying to solve the problem, we have scenes that offer greater insight to their character. In *Miracle Fish*, the boy delights in eating all the snacks he wants in the "Top Shop" without having to pay for them. He also loves taking as many stickers as he chooses. For a boy of impoverished means, these are both heightened moments. In *I Love Sarah Jane*, our character, Jimbo, asks Sarah, "Do you ever wonder if a fish feels the pain when it's hooked?" And we see the subtext of him asking if zombies feel pain when they're being impaled.

(8) MIDPOINT

Just as in a feature film, there's always a midpoint. It's a pivotal structural beat because the movie takes a dramatic turn at this moment and the plot is shifted into a new direction. In *Miracle Fish*, the midpoint is when we see a bloody handprint that reveals that danger lurks nearby and the fun and games are over. But there's dramatic irony because we've seen the fingerprints but the boy hasn't. In *I Love Sarah Jane*, Jimbo reveals to Sarah Jane that his family's dead, and for the first time, he seems to have gotten through to Sarah Jane; this hits her hard. She even allows Jimbo to put his arm around her. At the midpoint, Jimbo is finally getting closer to his goal of winning Sarah Jane's love.

(9) OBSTACLES

At this point, our story needs obstacles from both internal and external sources. In *I Love Sarah Jane*, the boys outside are intensifying their zombie attacks by pouring a gasoline mixture on a chained-up zombie so that they can blow him up by shooting a fire-arrow at him.

(10) RAISE THE STAKES

What is happening to your protagonist should feel like a life or death situation, whether it's emotionally or physically. In *Miracle Fish*, we know that the boy is alone and there's a killer loose. Tension builds. In *I love Sarah Jane*, Sarah is furious with the boys for blowing up the zombie. The film reveals that the zombie who's been chained up is her father—but he's still alive.

(11) PROMISE OF THE PREMISE

The promise of the premise refers to those scenes that make the most of the premise. This is when we deliver the laughs, the screams, or the tears. In *Miracle Fish*, the problem and the premise is that this boy is all alone, so we'd want to have scenes showing us what the boy would do if he were *really alone*. In *I Love Sarah Jane*, these are the scenes where we see Jimbo slowly getting closer with Sarah Jane, the love of his life.

(12) THE UNEXPECTED/END OF ACT TWO

There's always a major turning point that moves our story into the final act. In *Miracle Fish*, this is when the phone rings. The boy picks up and he's immediately asked if he can get to safety. It's clear that he's talking to a police officer and he's in dire straits. What's most important about Act Two is that our hero is even farther from solving his problem. In fact, he's in the worst trouble that he's been in in the entire movie. In *I Love Sarah Jane*, Sarah Jane's father bites the main bully. Jimbo watches cautiously and he's unsure if he's now lost Sarah Jane.

THIRD ACT BEATS

(13) BATTLE

How does the protagonist face off against the forces of antagonism? This can be an actual physical battle or an emotional battle. In *Miracle Fish*, the killer that we've been waiting for finally reveals himself, but we don't see him at first—we only hear him. And it's haunting. The battle is visceral in *I Love Sarah Jane* as she grabs a shovel and (offscreen) kills the bully, asking him if he's "out of his fucking misery."

(14) CONVERGENCE

In the third act, there's a convergence where everything that we've been waiting for finally comes together. Sometimes this means that all the characters we've met in the movie suddenly come together. In *Miracle Fish*, we finally meet the killer we've been waiting to see, and he enters the room with the boy. The killer is terrifying with his bloody shirt and shotgun in hand. In *I Love Sarah Jane*, we watch as Sarah Jane kills the zombie that's been chained up since the beginning of the movie. And even though he was a zombie, he was also Sarah Jane's father.

(15) WHAT IS THE LESSON LEARNED?

In *Miracle Fish*, the boy stays calm as he offers his fish toy to the killer. Perhaps the biggest lesson we learn from this moment is kindness. If we take the time to treat others with dignity, we'll be treated well in return, even if we're dealing with a psychotic killer. It's interesting that the theme in *I Love Sarah Jane* is also kindness. Jimbo, our protagonist, is in love with Sarah Jane. And the way he wins her over is through kindness.

(16) RESOLUTION/OPEN ENDING

In the last scene of *Miracle Fish*, we see a sharpshooter kill the villain. The boy is rescued and all seems to be okay with the world. But we know that the boy is forever changed. Will he continue to be a loner? Or will he have newfound status as the boy who survived a deadly situation? Who knows? That's the beauty of short films: they are often open-ended which opens the door for thoughtful discussion. In the last scene of *I Love Sarah Jane,* Sarah Jane retreats back upstairs to her house. But as she's walking up the stairs, she turns back to look at Jimbo as if to say, "Are you coming?" And Jimbo has the faintest of smiles, but the movie ends before we see what he does.

develop your short film

In the space below, begin to develop your short film idea.

1. Write down your logline.

2. Make a list of the scenes in your short film and number them.

3. Identify the key structural beats: inciting incident, midpoint, end of act 2, resolution.

4. Then on the next page, write up a brief summary of the film in prose.

summarize your film

Write a summary of your short film in prose.
Separate the summary in three paragraphs.
One paragraph for each act of your film.

DEVELOPING THE SHORT SCREENPLAY

1 OPENING

You want to draw the reader into the world. Establish the tone. Open visually. What are we seeing?

2 DEFINING ACTION

What is the protagonist doing when we first meet them? This establishes their character.

3 EXPOSITION

Who? What? When? Where? Are we...

4 SOMETHING HAPPENS

In a short: something disrupts the protagonist's routine and kicks the story into gear.

5 CONFLICT

You always want scenes of conflict in the story...

6 MIDDLE OF YOUR STORY

In an undefined number of scenes in a short film... make sure scenes push the story forward...

7 REVEAL CHARACTER INSIGHT or PROVIDE INFORMATION TO THE AUDIENCE

8 MID-POINT

9 OBSTACLES

Should present themselves from Internal and External Sources.

10 RAISE THE STAKES

What is happening to your protagonist should feel like a life or death situation. Either emotionally or physically.

11 THE PROMISE OF THE PREMISE

Deliver the laughs, screams, and tears throughout.

12 THE UNEXPECTED

Keep spinning the story in a new direction.

13 BATTLE

How does the protagonist face off against the forces of antagonism?

14 CONVERGENCE

Where is the final battle taking place?

15 WHAT IS THE LESSON LEARNED?

16 RESOLUTION/ OPEN ENDING

How do you want the audience to feel at the end?

145

break down a short film

Use the boxes below for the short film, *Validation*. You can find it on YouTube.

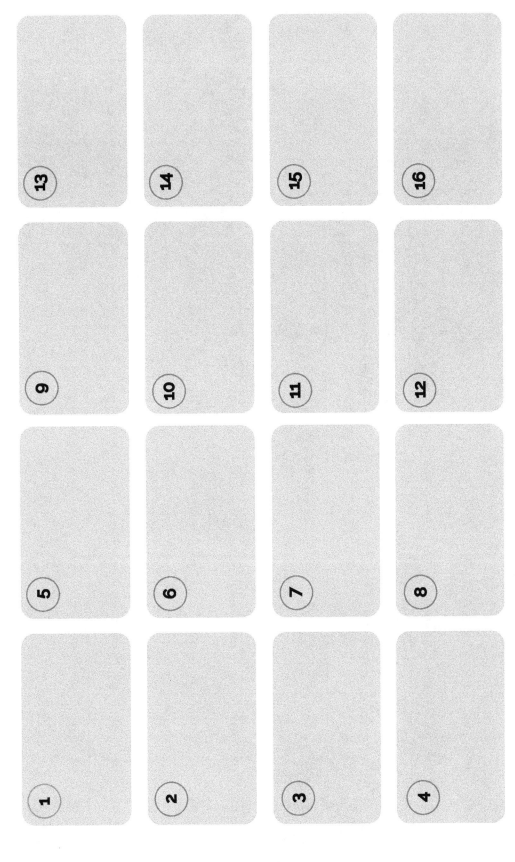

① 1

② 2

③ 3

④ 4

⑤ 5

⑥ 6

⑦ 7

⑧ 8

⑨ 9

⑩ 10

⑪ 11

⑫ 12

⑬ 13

⑭ 14

⑮ 15

⑯ 16

CHAPTER 9

Writing (and Formatting) the First Draft

THE IMPORTANCE OF SCRIPT FORMATTING

Before you are ready to write the first draft you need to feel as though you can't stand another minute breaking your story. You must feel as though you're bursting to write script pages and that you know your characters and the problem that they must solve in your story. The beauty of spending so much time developing your story is that when you finally sit down with your screenplay program, you will never experience writer's block. After all, as Steve Martin once said, "Writer's block is a fancy term made up by whiners so they can have an excuse to drink alcohol."

But there's just one last thing before you begin writing: you need to understand proper screenplay formatting. A film executive once told us that when she's reading a script, she puts it down if it's not properly formatted. She feels the same way about typos and grammatical errors. So even if you have a killer story, chances are the reader might never discover it because they'll be too frustrated by the improper formatting and grammatical errors.

So, what are the most important things to know about formatting? The easiest way to explain this is to open up the screenplay software programs. Back in the dark ages, before these existed, the writer had to count out the spaces and manually indent to the proper spot on the page. But if you were lucky enough to sell your script, the studio typists would take your script and actually re-type it so that it fits their proper margins.

But it's not the twentieth century—you've got script software and it's time to learn how to use it! We personally like Final Draft, Fade In, and Writer Duet, but that's not to say that you can't use another program. Final Draft is particularly good if you're a student because for the first eighteen weeks, you get to use it for free. And Final Draft and Fade In both offer discounted prices for students wishing to purchase their software. Writer Duet is great because it can be free or you can use another edition that they charge for.

We tell our students that screenwriting is like swimming in a lap pool. Here's why: one page of a screenplay = one minute of screen time. Now, given that most dramas are two hours (120 minutes), we know that most screenplays can't be more than 120 pages. A comedy or horror film is typically even shorter, so the expectation is about 105 pages. If you know you have to tell your story in 105 or 120 pages, then you've got to write within the confines of those prescribed pages—hence the lap pool. In contrast, novel writing is like swimming in the ocean—you can tell your story in as many pages as you choose. If it's a young adult novel, you might have 200 pages. If you're Michael Crichton, it's usually around 400 pages and then there's Tolstoy, who used just over 1,000 pages. The key is to remember that you don't have the novelist's prerogative or ability to use an infinite number of pages to tell your story. Because of this, you will have to write accordingly. And we'll need to use proper formatting.

If we think of a script as a blueprint, the formatting will clue us into the locations, the actors in the scene, the props needed, sound effects needed, and so much more. Like in the lyrics of "Do-Re-Mi" from *The Sound of Music*, "Let's start at the very beginning." At the beginning of any script is a scene heading.

Scene Heading

This tells us the location of the scene and whether it's indoors or outdoors as well as if it's night or day. INT = interior. EXT = exterior. The scene heading is arranged in the order of general to specific. So, if we have a basement scene in a haunted mansion that takes place during the day, it would look like this:

INT. HAUNTED MANSION — BASEMENT — DAY

And if we wanted a nighttime scene in the garden of the mansion, it would read like this:

EXT. HAUNTED MANSION — GARDEN — NIGHT

Notice that there is one space after the "EXT" and the period. And there's only one space on either side of the dashes. This may seem persnickety, but it's the requisite screenplay formatting. And when you don't follow it, the writing looks messy.

In more rare instances, we might want to indicate that the scene takes place both inside and outside. This sometimes happens in car sequences. If we are writing a car chase where the story cuts rapidly from inside to outside the car, the scene heading would look like this:

INT./EXT. CAR — NIGHT

What's important to understand is that EVERY TIME you change a location in your story, you need to type in a scene heading. In most script software programs, you can easily type in a new scene heading by tapping ENTER twice, and the cursor will move left on the page, knowing that you are ready to type in a new scene heading. At that point, the software will automatically put whatever you write into all capital letters to fit the format. However, it will not help you to properly arrange the words in the scene heading. You'll need to do that yourself. Below are some incorrect examples of scene headings followed by the correct version.

| #1 | INT.BEDROOM — HOUSE — NIGHT |
| | INT. HOUSE — BEDROOM — NIGHT |

| #2 | INT. — HOUSE — BEDROOM — NIGHT |
| | INT. HOUSE — BEDROOM — NIGHT |

| #3 | EXT — DRIVEWAY — HOUSE — DAY |
| | EXT. HOUSE — DRIVEWAY — DAY |

Once we've let our reader know where the scene takes place, we need to begin telling our story using action blocks.

Action Blocks

When we're writing the action, software programs will automatically make the prose single-spaced. The key is to keep these blocks to no more than three to four lines. Why? Because it's easier on the eye, making it a faster read. Large blocks of scene description are a death sentence to the new writer. Once you've completed your screenplay, one of your biggest challenges will be to get someone to read your script. And when that happens, you'll want to be sure that they read the *entire* script. Breaking up your action blocks and making the script an enjoyable read will aid you in your quest to get your movie made.

Another turn-off for the reader is when the script is littered with camera directions such as *wide shot, close-up, low angle, medium shot,* or *tracking shot.* Sure, you may have an idea of how you want your story to look, but there are better ways to indicate that in your script. One such way is to write, "we see . . ." because that tells the reader what you want them to focus on. We can also use a SHOT to alert our reader to something important.

Shot

All screenplay software programs have this option. The easiest way to access the shot function is to go to the dropdown bar and click on "SHOT." Then the cursor will move to the next line and put whatever you type into all capital letters, which will draw emphasis to your story. It's also a way to indicate a character's point-of-view (POV). Let's suppose we have a scene where a character named Bob gets a breakup letter from his girlfriend. Here are some shots that we could use in the writing of such a scene.

ON BOB'S FACE (this tells us it's a close-up on Bob's face)

BOB'S POV (this tells us that what we're seeing now is from Bob's point-of-view)

ON THE LETTER (this tells us we are looking at a close-up of the letter)

ANGLE ON BOB (this also tells us we're looking at Bob)

A shot is also useful when you're writing a big action scene and you have no dialogue. Since each page of a screenplay needs to equal one minute of screen time, we know that we're going to need to break up the action blocks so that one page of a script doesn't suddenly equal two minutes of screen time. Here's how we can break it up:

The car races down the highway. It roars over broken glass.

THE TIRES WOBBLE

The car slams into a partition.

CHARACTERS

Sooner or later someone is going to speak. A character's name always precedes their dialogue so we know who is speaking. The first time that a character is physically present in a scene in your script, you want to put their name in all capital letters. But if we first see a character in a photo or hear them offscreen, we don't put their name in capital letters. That doesn't happen until we actually see them in the scene. The reasoning for this rule goes back to the idea that a screenplay is a blueprint and it helps the actors and the assistant directors who are responsible for making up the schedule know where a particular actor first appears in a movie.

When we introduce these characters, we want to do it in a specific and compelling way that entices our reader. This is when it's okay to editorialize, or to tell us something we might not know from watching the screen. Yes, this is when you can break that HDWK (how do we know) rule.

When writing a character description, there are four things that we focus on: Name, age, occupation and their attitude toward life. Their relationship to other characters in the scene is sometimes included as well.

Let's introduce a boat-builder named Nate Waters. Having the first name begin with the letter N may be reminiscent of Noah from the Bible. The last name Waters drives the similarity home even further. You should never give your characters random names. Always make sure they mean something to your character and your story.

In addition, have all the character names in your script begin with a different letter. This helps your reader to avoid confusion about who is who. Imagine that we wrote a scene with four women named Jane, Janice, June and Julie. It's going to be hard to keep track of those four women. It would be much better to have them named Jane, Kate, Lisa, and Mary.

Let's return to the character description of Nate Waters. Since it's the first time we're meeting Nate, we'll put his name in all caps. If Nate is a fifty-year-old pessimistic boat builder, we'd write it like this:

NATE WATERS (50), is a boat builder who is convinced that the world is coming to an end. His age will probably be clear to us from watching this scene, and chances are, we'll know his occupation because he could be building a boat when we first meet him. However, it would be impossible to know that he thinks the world is coming to an end just from looking at him. We also wouldn't know his name unless there's dialogue or he's wearing a nametag, and it adds to our story if we tell our reader these bits of information. After the character introduction, try to stick to the images that tell us what we're seeing on the screen.

Dialogue

Formatting dialogue is straightforward using script software programs. It's as easy as hitting TAB on your keyboard and the cursor will indent to the proper location. Or you can click on the dropdown bar that's labeled "Dialogue." But before you write the dialogue, you need to write the character's name. To do this you hit TAB (or the dropdown labeled "Character") and then you type in the character's name that will automatically be put into all CAPITAL LETTERS. Then you hit RETURN and the cursor will automatically indent to the proper margin for dialogue. That's really all there is to it.

Parentheticals

What becomes complicated with formatting dialogue is when you choose to use PARENTHET-ICALS. Parentheses are used when you want to *describe* how a person speaks. This can include whispers, coughs, screams, stutters, and more. It shouldn't be used to describe action. Here are some examples:

BETTINA
(whispers)
We shouldn't be here.

Notice that whatever we write in parentheticals must be in lower case. Using capital letters is incorrect unless the word is a proper noun. This is one of those picky rules, however, we must follow it. Otherwise it looks like amateur hour. Here are some incorrect examples of using parentheticals followed by the last and most correct example.

TYLER
(YELLS)
Get out of here now!

TYLER
(yells)
Get out of here now!

TYLER
GET OUT OF HERE NOW!

Notice that the last example which has Tyler yelling shows that there's no parentheticals. If a character is screaming or yelling, it's acceptable to put their dialogue in all capital letters—that way, you don't even need to use the parentheses.

Parentheticals can also be used when you want to indicate to whom a character is talking. This is helpful when part of the dialogue is addressed to one person, and then the other part is spoken to someone else. For example:

BETTINA
Formatting is an important part of screenwriting.
(to Bob)
Please put away your phone.
(to Class)
I hope this is all making sense.

You could also avoid using parentheses in the above example by writing it this way:

BETTINA
Formatting is an important part of screenwriting.

Bettina turns to Bob. She sees him texting.

BETTINA
Please put away your phone.

Bettina turns back to the rest of the class. She forces a smile.

BETTINA
I hope this is all making sense.

Note: the first example is better because we have more "white on the page," so it's easier to read. The second example is clumsier because it's a slower read, and when the read gets slow, that's when the reader puts down the script. Then your script never gets made into a movie! And finally, a parenthetical is used best when used least. Let the dialogue and the scene explain the quality.

Phone Calls

It's important to indicate when your character is talking on the phone. Here's the easiest way:

RYAN
(into phone)
I'll see you later. Maybe around ten.

If you have two characters talking on the phone and they are in different locations, it's awkward to constantly write in a "scene heading" each time we cut from one person to the other. In this case, it's acceptable to write:

Ryan and Ava talk on the phone. We intercut between them as necessary.

Text Messages

To be honest, there's no one rule for how to write a text message in a screenplay. Texting is still relatively new in the world of screenwriting, especially since it didn't become popular until the early 2000s. The easiest way to write a text message in a script is to write it like the dialogue for a phone call. One exception is that the message itself is written in *italics*. For example:

Sabrina looks at her phone.

AVA (TEXT)
OMG. Where are you?

Sabrina frowns, quickly thumbs a response.

SABRINA (TEXT)
B right thr.

You can also write the text messages in bold. Texts are now visualized when they pop-up on the screen. This is becoming more mainstream. We have seen it in *House of Cards*, *Fruitvale Station*, and *Sherlock*.

OTHER FORMATTING QUESTIONS—IT'S THE STORY, STUPID

The truth is that once you begin to write a script, you will probably have questions about formatting. The reality is that at some point there is more than one way to format a script. So when in doubt, choose the way that best tells your story and tells it in a way that doesn't confuse the reader. At the end of the day, if it's a strong story, a minor mistake in formatting won't hurt you.

Writer's Block

So you've developed your story for as long as you can and you've started to write. In spite of all your best plans, you hit the big WB. Not Warner Bros, Writers Block. What's a young writer to do? Consider your writing habits.

WRITING HABITS

Take out a Sharpie and write down the following rules on index cards:

Write each day.
Write at the same time each day.
Even an hour is good.
Don't write your entire script in one sitting.

Now put a cap on that Sharpie and consider the following:

1. **CARRY A NOTEBOOK WITH YOU**
   Always write down new ideas. Then every so often, copy what you've written in that notebook onto a file in your computer that we like to label "Well." Don't assume that you'll remember a great idea, because you won't and you'll be sad when that happens.

2. **HAVE A DRIVING REASON TO WRITE**
   Create a desire for yourself (it shouldn't be to make a million dollars), because screenwriting is a long process and if you have no particular need to tell this story, it's going to come up empty or meaningless and be tinged with a lack of authenticity. This ties in with knowing the theme of your story, which should be the answer to why you want to tell it.

3. **BELIEVE YOU'RE TALENTED ENOUGH**
   Don't listen to that annoying voice in your head that says you're not good enough. Silence your inner critic. When you're writing that first draft, it's all too easy to listen to the negative voice and stop writing. Sure, most of the first draft might not be great, but there will be some jewels even if it's just a few lines of dialogue.

4. **BE ENTHUSIASTIC AND PASSIONATE ABOUT THE CRAFT OF SCREENWRITING**
Thanks to the Internet there's no shortage of professional scripts to read online. In fact, before you begin writing, it's always a good idea to open up a professional script and read at least a few pages. This will put you in the proper frame of mind to write a script and not a novel. Screenplay writing has a specific style of its own and the best way to wrap your head around this is to read! Watch the movies that you want to emulate. Know their genre.

5. **BE COMMITTED**
Understand that becoming a writer doesn't mean that it's just about one screenplay. It's the third, fourth, or fifth screenplay you write. The sooner you write your first, the sooner you will be onto writing your second script.

6. **CREATE A DEDICATED WRITING SPACE**
Find a specific place where you can consistently write. This can be at a desk or a kitchen table or the foot of your bed—whatever works for you! And once this space is created, whenever you sit down at the location your brain will tell you that it's time to write. When you try to write in different locations, your brain will find a reason to have writer's block. Consistency improves creativity.

7. **BE A WRITER**
Don't be someone who talks about writing or plans to write.
Don't be someone who says they have a great idea in their head.
Don't be someone who writes five pages and quits.

8. **WRITE TO MUSIC**
This works particularly well when you listen to the same music over and over, as it can be a trigger for your brain to realize that it's time to write (just like your location). When you write to music, your brain increases its creativity quotient. And best of all, what you're writing suddenly sounds brilliant and it will be a real morale-booster. So try loading up Pandora or Spotify on your computer. Some of our favorite soundtracks to write to include: "Honor Him" from *Gladiator*, "Forrest Gump Suite" from *Forrest Gump*, "Roots and Beginnings" from *The Lord of the Rings*, and if you need a very long soundtrack, try James Horner's "Titanic Suite" from the *Titanic* soundtrack.

9. **ACCEPT THAT THE FIRST DRAFT WILL BE TERRIBLE**
Some screenwriters call it the "garbage draft" or the "vomit draft." Others call it the "s*&# first draft." Whatever you call it, it's something that just needs to be written. Once you've got that first draft, you will start to find the pearls when you re-write. After all, screenwriting is re-writing.

10. BE ABLE TO STATE THE DRAMATIC QUESTION OF YOUR MOVIE

If you can't do this, then you're not ready to write. Having a dramatic question implies there will be conflict and structure in your story. According to the great, late screenwriting guru Syd Field, "All drama is conflict. Without conflict, you have no action. Without action, you have no character. Without character, you have no story. And without story, you ain't got no screenplay."

writing the first draft

KEEP A WRITING SCHEDULE

Write every day! Keep track of your writing.

**WRITE TO MUSIC. LIST THREE SONGS
OR SOUNDTRACKS THAT INSPIRE YOU WHILE WRITING:**

1. _____

2. _____

3. _____

poster time

MAKE A POSTER FOR YOUR MOVIE!
In the space below, draw the poster for your short film.
If you despise drawing, cut out images and paste them to the space.

formatting

Write the Scene Headings for the following locations. Be sure to use dashes and periods properly.

1. Parking lot of a restaurant at night.

2. Museum bathroom during the day.

3. Bridge of a spaceship at night.

4. Campfire in the woods at night.

5. Operating room of a hospital during the day.

6. Supply closet of the English office in a university during the day.

7. House driveway at night.

8. A car driving on the highway during the day.

9. A flashback scene in a girl's bedroom at night.

10. A dream sequence in a forest during the day.

ANSWERS PROVIDED ON THE FOLLOWING PAGE.

formatting | ANSWERS

1 Parking lot of a restaurant at night.

EXT. RESTAURANT - PARKING LOT - NIGHT

2 Museum bathroom during the day.

INT. MUSEUM - BATHROOM - DAY

3 Bridge of a spaceship at night.

EXT. SPACESHIP - BRIDGE - NIGHT

4 Campfire in the woods at night.

EXT. WOODS - CAMPFIRE - NIGHT

5 Operating room of a hospital during the day.

INT. HOSPITAL - OPERATING ROOM - DAY

6 Supply closet of the English office in a university during the day.

INT. UNIVERSITY - ENGLISH OFFICE - SUPPLY CLOSET - DAY

7 House driveway at night.

EXT. HOUSE - DRIVEWAY - NIGHT

8 A car driving on the highway during the day.

INT./EXT. HIGHWAY - CAR - DAY

9 A flashback scene in a girl's bedroom at night.

INT. GIRL'S BEDROOM - NIGHT- FLASHBACK

10 A dream sequence in a forest during the day.

EXT. FOREST - DAY - DREAM SEQUENCE

CHAPTER 10

Giving and Getting Notes

Kiss, Kick, Kiss

Giving notes and getting notes can break the heart of a new screenwriter. Some development executives and agents are terrible at giving notes; they will only talk about what they hated and not have any idea of how to help the writer fix the script. We promote peer-to-peer critiques of work because we want writers to learn to not overreact to notes. Writers should also ask questions but try to not be defensive. If you are ever in a meeting with an executive and you're confronted with the most absurd note ever, you don't want to tell them that they gave you a stupid note. You want to work. You want to have a reputation as someone the studio or network can work with on other projects. You might respond to the crazy executive in this manner: "That's an interesting idea. Let me see where it goes." Let them know you are giving their idea the respect they think it deserves.

Your fellow students deserve that same level of respect. Remember, the students who are in your classroom now might be the ones in a position to buy your material later in your career.

You want to get multiple reads on your script. Every writer has their group of "beta-testers"—other creatives to whom they can trust and give their early drafts.

You are going to hate the notes—or at least some of them. You don't have to take and implement everyone's notes (even if you are on assignment for a network or a studio), but you should still listen to them. Our rule has always been that if you hate the note, ignore it. However, if you keep hearing the same note over again, then maybe you should listen. Keep in mind:

If you keep hearing the same note—you have a problem.
If you keep rejecting the same note—you have a problem.

When it comes to giving notes on material, some agencies and studios teach a "kiss, kick, kiss" approach.

First you KISS, which is a nice thing. Find something positive to say about the material. Find a nugget or a morsel that worked for you.

Then you KICK; this is where you deliver the constructive notes of what *didn't* work for you and why. Never say "It wasn't for me," or, "It's not my type of story." A lot of wannabe writers become great development executives or producers, and because there are so many creative outlets for storytellers, they have to be open to all ideas. You want to be prepared when giving notes, so read the script. Where did it slow down? Why did you hate the main character? Be honest. If the writing is sloppy, you can say that the style of writing interfered with the read, the typos were distracting, or that the large blocks of text made it hard to read.

Finally, you come back with another KISS which suggests that either the writer or the project has promise. You can bring it back to the writing room if you do the work, with a re-write or three, you have a chance at something.

NOTES YOU MIGHT HEAR

"It's not for me."

We don't say that, but unfortunately not everyone in Hollywood has read this book. This note means that the reader/audience could not connect with the material. Go back and look for the primal emotion that grounds the material. In the Mike Birbiglia indie comedy *Don't Think Twice*, we are in the world of improv. But what is primal is the jealousy each member of the troupe feels when one of their own breaks into fame and success. The film also includes themes of love, death, pregnancy, and the fear of failure—all of which are primal emotions. Make sure your story has something at its core that everyone can relate to.

"I don't like the main character."

Often this comes about because the reader/audience does not understand the motivation of the main character. Do you change point-of-views in the story? Do we see the main character talking to other people? Even in *Captain America: Civil War*, the characters are continually talking about why they're acting the way they are acting. Express. Emote. Explain.

"I didn't understand it."

This note might be a result of a complicated plot. We had a student telling a story with dual narratives. One story takes place in the present and the other in the 1800s, but the surprise ending was that the 1800s story was really taking place in 1950. We were very confused and asked them why they did it that way. Often this note occurs because the writer is trying to be overly clever with their plot. This can work very well (*Memento, The Sixth Sense, The Usual Suspects),* but those writers worked and reworked their scripts so that there was only one big hook that turned everything. We see writers put too many twists and turns in their stories that result in dramatic whiplash.

"I got bored."

This is an honest note. You want to keep the audience involved? Ask yourself if you're giving them too little information. Every story is a mystery, and the questions about, and in the story, push the reader/audience forward. Pose questions for them, and they might want to stay around for the answer. Something like: *Is she really going to shoot him on their wedding day?*

Another cause of boredom might be that the scenes, or entirety of the script, are too long. Not every little detail is necessary. Today's audiences have seen and/or read so many stories. It's a time of personal narrative, so keep it short. Every script is different. One of the criticisms of the second season of a Netflix comedy is that the first season had twenty-two minute episodes. But the second season episodes were close to twice that long.

"What's it supposed to be about?"

Sometimes the lack of thematic resonance can kill a story. Have something to say. Look at the short film *The Hunter and the Swan Discuss Their Meeting.* A Brooklyn couple has dinner with a hunter and his girlfriend, a magical swan woman. It doesn't go well. Written and directed by Emily Carmichael, the story is really about how it doesn't matter what way a couple meets. What matters is what happens after.

"It didn't feel like a movie or show I'd want to see."

This means that you didn't do your job as writer. You wrote a script, not a movie or TV show, which means that you were not visual enough. The reader/audience did not see the movie in their head. One solution is to "track the transitions." How do you go from scene to scene? In *Raiders of the Lost Ark,* as the Nazis are pulling away with the ark, Indiana says to his ally, Sallah, "Meet me at Omar's. Be ready for me. I'm going after that truck."

Sallah wonders, "How?"

Indiana doesn't explain his plan. He doesn't let the audience know what is going to happen next. He says famously, "I don't know, I'm making this up as I go!"

The next scene begins with Indy riding a horse chasing Nazis and their tank armada as people cheer.

The transition keeps the story moving. Often the transition or the shot conveys information that the audience has to put together on their own. No one expresses what is happening on the screen—instead, we see it onscreen.

Take a look at the short film, *It All Goes Away.* According to the website iO9, the film, which was directed by Zachariah Smith, is based on *Sam's Story,* from Superman/Batman #26 by Jeph Loeb and with contributions by his son, Sam. The story sees Superman recount the first time he first truly experienced loss on Earth: the death of a close friend from his high school years, who had cancer. The real Sam Loeb, who suffered from bone cancer, passed away at the age of seventeen before the issue ran. When the story was published it was inundated with contributions from a bevy of industry writers and artists—in memory of him.[1]

The story is about cancer and death. It is also one of the best Superman stories told on film. Those two moments in the story are huge: we show the film and ask the students to tell us where in the film Sam tells Clark that he has cancer.

There is no scene like that. Clark uses his "x-ray" vision to see there is something wrong with Sam's leg. Later, Sam comes to finally tell Clark, but we don't see or hear the whole scene. We cut away to Clark's reaction with his father. The "I have cancer" scene is never on the screen.

Later, when Sam dies, we don't see an overdramatic deathbed scene. We see Clark in school and a scene of silence as a teacher talks to the class. Clark looks over at the empty seat next to him, and that visual information conveys the death of Sam. The audience is allowed to figure out what has happened.

Rewrite and Format for Style and Storytelling

Technical format errors should never occur. But we see them with scene descriptions and character names too frequently. Some format errors are very basic "by the book" errors. Remember your script is meant to be enjoyed. The first time people are considering it they want to have a visceral experience. They want to swipe to the last page and feel as if they have seen a television show or a movie. So don't always overdo with the technical formatting, especially with scene headings.

As you re-write, look for moments in the script that are those big "close-up" moments. Remember no camera directions should be in your script. In our opinion, it breaks the wall and reminds the reader that they are reading a screenplay. You want them watching the movie no one's made yet.

You can direct the reader on the rewrite by formatting for style and storytelling. This was covered in the chapter on visual storytelling. But now as you re-write your script, you are looking for more of these moments.

As you read each paragraph of scene description, make sure you don't bury the lead. Either start the two to three lines of scene description with the most important thing, or better yet, end the paragraph with the most important thing in that paragraph.

For example:

> A flashlight beam sprays the room. He passes Jerome's body, on the ground twitching. The stake through his heart. Jerome rises. Steve walks into the pockets of the darkness.

The last line is meaningless to the drama. Jerome is rising from the dead and Steve is just walking around. You can move "Steve walks into the pockets . . ." earlier, which leaves the dead body rising as the turning point of the scene description.

> A flashlight beam sprays the room. Steve walks into the pockets of the darkness. He passes Jerome's body, on the ground twitching. The stake through his heart. Jerome rises . . .

You can go even further and direct the reader by using a SLUGLINE for description. When the movie is prepped for production, the production manager or assistant will do the technical pass on formatting to make sure that all of the scene headings are correct. But for now, you want to sell that story. So make sure you have emotion in your re-write.

> A flashlight beam sprays the room. Steve walks into the pockets of the darkness. He passes Jerome's body, on the ground twitching. The stake through his heart. And then . . .

> JEROME RISES

We added the words "And then . . ." setting up the reader and making sure that "Jerome rises" is in caps on a separate line in case the reader missed it. We also wanted to dictate the shot.

You should also break up scene descriptions as you re-write. You want to avoid giant blobs of text in the scene description and the dialogue. If you have a long monologue, intercut it with action. Remember your action verbs. Characters are always doing something, even if it's getting a shave or making a cup of coffee. A character that just stands, sits, drives, or talks can border on boring.

Look at the end of *The Incredibles*: Mr. Incredible faces off against Syndrome. Syndrome starts "monologuing"—giving us a lot of exposition. But he's not just standing there performing this monologue; he is physically attacking Mr. Incredible. We also see quick FLASH CUTS back to this early life. If you have a large chunk of dialogue, you should expand the visual language in the re-write.

Hunt for the HDWK's (How Do We Know Moments). They are found in the script of a new screenwriter. They tell us information rather than show us that information. For example:

> Bill, a down-on-his-luck alcoholic whose wife and kids left, has not eaten in days. He just lost his job where he used to make a lot of money. He searches a trash can for food.

There is no way to know all that about Bill from the image. The writer has told us. But you can't film it. You can't see it.

You want to eliminate all HDWK's. You can use editorializing to convey mood and attitude as long as you don't use it all the time.

> A middle-aged man sweats in an Armani suit in need of a dry cleaner. He searches a trash can. Spies a half-eaten Taco Bell burrito at the bottom. He leans in and vomits. Then—retrieves the burrito. He uses his two hundred dollar stained tie as a napkin to clean off his own bile. This is BILL. He used to be rich, not so much these days.

Are You Writing the Right Scenes?

You want to redo a scene list based on what you have written. Chances are, you veered away from your original outline. This is not a bad thing. It means that you were immersed in your story and you followed your characters. You heard their voice and became a fly on the wall in your story.

Make a scene list of what you have written and identify the scenes. Is the scene a big event or a turning point that causes the story to spin into another direction? Does the scene lead to an unexpected moment? Is there a surprising reveal that turns the scene and the characters?

Once you identify those, look at what comes before and after that big event. For example, let's say the big event is a wedding. Do we see a scene of the bride and groom preparing for the big event? Are guests arriving? These are scene of preparations, and they're very important because it allows the audience to share in the character's point-of-view.

"Why are you marrying this guy?"
"I can't believe you finally are getting married!"
Or as Vince Vaughn says in *Old School* as the bride heads down the aisle: "Run."

Scenes of preparation might also be scenes of bank robbers getting ready to rob a bank as in *Heat.* It can be a lawyer prepping for a huge courtroom battle. It can be the fighter getting ready for the fight like in *Creed.* In *Sully,* Sully and the passengers prepare for an emergency landing on the Hudson. It leads to a tense harrowing event, which is the landing.

Now look at the scene that happens *after* a big event. Do you have a reaction scene? Are the characters reacting to the couple getting married ("I give them five months")? Did people die in the bank robbery? Sully is hailed as a hero but he is troubled with doubts. These are the reaction or aftermath scenes. We want to see your characters reacting to the events.

In the Oscar-winning short film *God of Love,* written and directed by Luke Matheny, the big midpoint event is a date that went badly. The next scene is our hero talking to his best friend about how bad it was. It also allows the characters to regroup, express emotion, and formulate a new plan to reach their goal. The best friend questions the plan time and time again. In this case, the best friend is asking the same questions as the audience, which leads us to the Greek Chorus.

Use "Greek Chorus" to stand in for an audience. Have your characters question the antagonist. Maybe have them question the protagonist. Why are they acting this way? What did they think was going to happen?

I HATE MY SCRIPT

Welcome to the world of being a writer. Writers hate the first draft of their scripts. But before you give it to anyone you need to clean up your own mess. You did it, it's your responsibility. There is no maid to clean it up—so do it.

There should be no typos in the script you send into the world. Nothing bothers a reader more than writers who are too lazy to clean up their own typos. A typo can lead to confusion. In the classic Woody Allen movie, *Take the Money and Run,* a typo on the bank robbery note leads to hilarity as the thief and the bank manager argue whether the word is "gun" or "gum."

Does it look like a script? If there are large blocks of text, break them up. In the days before PDFs, the delivery system of material included messengers that would bike or drive around Los Angeles delivering scripts. The executive would be able to hold up the script and have an idea of what was in their hands. The script might feel heavy. They would look at the page count and see 135 pages from a new writer.

Pass.

They now swipe through and see if there are large globs of text and dialogue.

Pass.

Do the work. Scripts are lean and concise. You are not explaining a story, you are showing a story.

Read the dialogue in your story out loud. We workshop most material in class. Students act out the parts and the writer has to listen—and cringe. Most student writers are not good actors, but you'd be surprised how much a good script can hide bad acting.

Also, print your dialogue for each character separately. Each character needs to sound different and have different attitudes to display different styles of speech.

THE SEVEN TRACKING PASSES

You are going to do more than one pass on your screenplay. As you re-write you want passes that concentrate on:

1. **STRUCTURAL PASS**—does the story move from scene to scene? Is there a clear beginning, middle, and end?

2. **EMOTIONAL PASS**—track the protagonist's emotional state from the beginning of the script to the end. Does the character change? Are you displaying different aspects of the characters in each scene?

3. **CHARACTERS PASS**—are the characters clear with their goals and motivation? Are they consistent?

4. **TRANSITION PASS**—do your transitions work from scene to scene? An overuse of CUT TO's drive us crazy. Save them for the big impact cuts.

5. **VISUAL PASS**—is the story visual? A trick is to set each scene with visuals. Show us three images to start the scene to get us in the mood. Do you tell us information rather than show us information? Someone yelling, "I got shot" is not as visual as seeing that in a scene.

6. **DIALOGUE PASS**—dialogue is the last thing to be polished. Go back and look at the traits assigned to your characters. If they are hot-headed, does their dialogue reflect that through the script?

7. **AUDIENCE PASS**—the question we always ask is, "How do you want the audience to feel after seeing this show or movie?" The characters in the story have their objective, but the writer has their own. Have you delivered on the promise of the premise and scared the audience in a horror movie? Have you made them laugh and learn in a comedy?

Scripts are not written, they are rewritten, and writing is not writing, it's re-writing. Once you get that first draft done, the work begins. Trust the work. Trust the process. What do you have in common with the most famous and productive writers in the history of film and television? You know that it is not easy. Every writer struggles with their story from its outline to the final passes.

You are not alone. Find or form a writer's group. Re-write your script and your life. One day at a time, one page at a time.

ENDNOTE

1. http://io9.gizmodo.com/this-fan-film-about-supermans-first-encounter-with-grie-1786849232

GIVING NOTES

There are many different ways to give notes but the best way is to give positive, constructive criticism. Here is an exercise for giving brief notes on a script.

KISS. KICK. KISS.

Kiss is a positive word. Kick is not. So if we use "Kick, Kick, Kiss" to give feedback on a script, it would be to list one positive thing followed by something that should be fixed and then ending on an upbeat note with something good about the script. Knowing what to keep is as important as knowing what to fix.

NAME: _____

KISS

KICK

KISS

NAME: _____

KISS

KICK

KISS

CHAPTER 11

Short Film, Long Career!

PROOF OF CONCEPT

Proof of concept is the term used in Hollywood that means an idea is already proven on another platform. For film executives, this means that the film or television project has a greater chance of being financially successful and thus executives can feel more secure about putting millions into a movie. Having a *proof of concept* gives you a far greater chance at having your project green-lit by a studio or private investors.

Let's consider what some of these other platforms might be.

The most common *proof of concept* is a book: fiction or non-fiction. *The Girl on a Train*, *The Big Short*, *Room*, *Brooklyn*, *Carol*, *The Martian*, *American Sniper*, *The Imitation Game*, *The Theory of Everything*, *The Wolf of Wall Street*, *Silver Linings Playbook*, *Life of Pi*, *No Country of Old Men*, *Seabiscuit*, *About a Boy*, *The Hours*, *The Lord of the Rings*, and *Gone Girl* are some of the more recent novel-to-film translations. The popular film *Mean Girls* was based on Rosalind Wiseman's non-fiction self-help book *Queen Bees and Wannabes*, which describes female high school social cliques and the damaging effects they can have on girls.[1] The Academy Awards even have a special category for these movies with the "Best Adapted Screenplay" award. While it's true that this category also applies to a play, television show, or short story, it is most often a script that's based on a novel. Young adult movies practically have a direct pipeline to Hollywood movies as we've seen with *Twilight*, *Divergent*, *Harry Potter*, *Hunger Games*, and almost every John Green young adult novel. Even e-books have turned into movies such as *Fifty Shades of Gray* and *Wool*.

Other common *proofs of concept* are comics and graphic novels. We need only to go to our local multiplex to verify this point. From *Superman*, *Batman*, *Spiderman*, *Avengers*, *Captain America*, *Iron Man*, *Men in Black*, *Suicide Squad*, *Wonder Woman*, and *Guardians of the Galaxy*, Hollywood believes that comics are guaranteed to be profitable. Basically every superhero movie was first a comic book or graphic novel. We have known producers who create new comics solely for the purpose of ensuring that their idea is already vetted on another platform. *The Walking Dead* is based on the Image Comics created by writer Robert Kirkman and artist Tony Moore.

True Stories are another popular *proof of concept*. Audiences love to flock to films about events that have actually happened. Even when we know the outcome, we glean some new fact about the actual event. We've seen this most recently in *Sully* and *Snowden*. Typically, these are known as biopics and they cover both newer subjects such as *Steve Jobs* to *Captain Phillips* to the past with *Trumbo, Lincoln,* and *12 Years a Slave*. Often these movies are based on historical periods and cover many individuals such as *Straight Outta Compton* and *Suffragette*.

In recent years, even video games have been turned into movies. This was inevitable as Hollywood watched their popularity grow and earn billions of dollars. In truth, there hasn't been a hugely successful film made from a video game. *Tomb Raider* was the most popular, spawning a sequel and now a reboot. Recent video game themed movies include: *Warcraft, Resident Evil,* and *Assassin's Creed*. Even the game *Minecraft* has been green-lit.

Board games have also been used as a *proof of concept* and without much financial success for Hollywood studios. These include the games *Clue* and *Battleship*. But unlike board games, toys have been a very successful *proof of concept* for films. We've seen this especially in the *Transformers* franchise and the many movies based on *American Girl Dolls*. The success of *G.I. Joe* led to a sequel and then to the inevitable *Transformers/G.I. Joe* crossover film which is now in development. These toy movies have been financially successful and they're escapist fun for both kids and adults.

Remakes of foreign films have long been *proof of concept* fodder for Hollywood films. From the numerous French comedies of Francois Veber, *La Cage aux Folles* remade as *The Birdcage,* to the Japanese *Ring* series, to *The Departed* which was based on Wai-Keung Lau's *Infernal Affairs*. Some other foreign remakes include *12 Monkeys, Father's Day, Down and Out in Beverly Hills, Three Men and a Baby,* and *Homeland* which is based on the Israeli series *Prisoners of War*.

Hollywood has even looked to theme parks as a proof of concept for their films. Their first forays into using theme parks as a proof of concept didn't fare well. In fact we're guessing that most people have never seen the movie *Country Bears* based on the Disney attraction, *Country Bear Jamboree*. And even with the star wattage of Eddie Murphy, the Disney movie *Haunted Mansion* was a flop. But Disney didn't give up as they finally hit pay dirt with the wildly successful franchise of *Pirates of the Caribbean* films based on the Disney ride of the same name.

THE STUDENT'S PROOF OF CONCEPT: THE SHORT FILM

Given that most students can't afford to buy the rights to a novel, comic book, or theme park ride, how can they jump on the *proof of concept* bandwagon? The answer is simple. It's the short film. And the advantage for students today is that thanks to the easy access to distribution on YouTube or Vimeo, it's easier than ever to get noticed with a short film. In her recent book, *Sleepless in Hollywood* (2014), Film Producer Linda Obst (*Interstellar, Contact, Hot in Cleveland, Sleepless in Seattle*) describes how agents and assistants spend their day. She says they're not reading scripts and meeting with producers and writers because that's old school. Instead they're looking online for short films and other new material. And these development executives are producers who are looking for both new individuals that they might want to work with and also ideas that might be developed into feature films or television programs.

What do the following names have in common? Jason Reitman, Guy Ritchie, Christopher Nolan. Before they were huge Hollywood directors, they all made short films first. And some were made during film school.

Why do short films work so well as a proof of concept? It's easy to see if a story can work dramatically in a short. Consider these short films that went on to become feature films.

RECENT SHORT FILMS THAT BECAME FEATURES

Lights Out (2016)

In 2013, Swedish filmmaker David Sandberg and his wife Lotta Losten created the short film *Lights Out* for the purpose of winning a film contest. Sandberg wrote and directed and his wife starred in the film. After not winning any awards, they posted the film on YouTube and Vimeo where it went viral. Soon Hollywood was calling and in short order they moved to Los Angeles where they teamed up with producers Lawrence Grey, James Wan, and Eric Heisserer to make a feature film version of the supernatural horror film, *Lights Out*. The film was made for just under $5 million and earned $145 million worldwide.

Whiplash (2014)

As described on IMDb, *Whiplash* tells the story of "a promising young drummer who enrolls at a cut-throat music conservatory where his dreams of greatness are mentored by an instructor who will stop at nothing to realize a student's potential."[2] *Whiplash* was originally a "Black List Script." According to Wikipedia, "The Black List is an annual survey of the 'most liked' motion picture screenplays not yet produced."[3] This list is generated by film development executives who vote on their favorite scripts of that particular year. But being a Black List Script wasn't enough to get the movie made. So the writer/director Damian Chazelle made a short film of the movie which was selected as a short film at Sundance in 2014. This short film attracted investors and thus, the feature film was then made from that Black Listed Script. The feature film of *Whiplash* premiered at Sundance in 2014 where Sony Classics bought the theatrical rights. The movie had a hugely successful theatrical run and was nominated for Best Picture and Best Adapted Screenplay and won three Academy Awards for Best Film Editing, Best Sound Mixing, and Best Supporting Actor.

Helion (2014)

Before *Helion* became a feature film, it premiered at the Sundance Film Festival in 2013 as a short film. Then in 2014, it premiered as a feature at the Sundance Film Festival. Sundance Selects then acquired the theatrical rights. As described on IMDb, *Helion is* "When motocross and heavy metal obsessed thirteen-year-old Jacob's increasing delinquent behavior forces CPS to place his little brother, Wes, with his aunt. Jacob and his emotionally absent father, Hollis, must finally take responsibility for their actions and for each other in order to bring Wes home."[4]

This Is the End (2013)

This feature film starring James Franco and Seth Rogen was originally based on the trailer of a short film called *Jay vs. Seth vs. The Apocalypse*. Wikipedia summarizes the movie as "two friends and actors who have shut themselves in their apartment and argue over their predicament during some unspecified end-of-the-world event."[5] In 2007, a trailer was made of the short and posted on YouTube where it quickly went viral and attracted the attention of several studios who wanted the rights for production. The irony is that the full short wasn't released until the feature film came out.[6]

Mama (2013)

In 2008, Andres Muschietti directed and co-wrote with his sister the 2008 Spanish language short film, *Mama*. This three-minute short caught the attention of renowned filmmaker Guillermo del Toro. According to YouTube, "the craftsmanship, ingenuity, and horror presented by the Muschiettis made him want to be a Producer for the feature film."[7] The feature film went into production in 2011 and was the first film that Muschietti directed. Upon its release *Mama* was not only a critical success, but also a huge financial hit as it grossed $146 million and was made for only $15 million.

Frankenweenie (2012)

In 1984, when Tim Burton was just twenty-five years old, and he was already working at Disney Studios, he made a short live action black and white film called *Frankenweenie*. The short film was about a young boy who sets out to revive his dead pet using science. According to *Slate*, Burton's short was supposed to be shown before the animated *Pinocchio* in its rerelease, but Disney shelved the two-minute short when the MPAA gave it a PG rating. Burton offered to try and make the film G rated but according to Burton, they said, "There's nothing you can cut, it's just the tone."[8] Of course the irony is that *Pinocchio* is perhaps just as scary, if not more so than the early *Frankenweenie*. Nonetheless, Disney shelved the short until 1992 when it was put on home video. Finally the film was realized twenty-eight years later as a stop motion animated feature in 2012 and was subsequently nominated for Best Animated Feature at the Academy Awards in 2013.

District 9 (2009)

According to the Internet site Premium Beat, *Alive in Joburg*, the short film that spawned *District 9*, is one of the best proof of concept films of all time.[9] In 2006, Neil Blomkamp wrote and directed the science fiction short in Johannesburg. The short caught the attention of producer Peter Jackson who helped to produce the feature version. *District 9* went on to garner several 2009 Academy Award nominations including Best Picture, Best Adapted Screenplay, Best Visual Effects, and Best Editing. Blomkamp's career was also ignited as he went on to direct *Elysium* and *Chappie*.

Half Nelson (2006)

Ryan Gosling was nominated for an Academy Award for his performance as a drug-addicted inner city teacher in the feature film, *Half Nelson* which is based on *Gowanus, Brooklyn*, the short film written by Ryan Fleck and Anna Boden. According to an interview with Ryan Fleck in *Filmmaker Magazine*, "we made the short as a tool to gain awareness for the feature. We shot it in the style very similar to the way we wanted to do *Half Nelson*. We ended up using the same lead actress, Shareeka Epps. And it worked out."[10] The short film did more than just work out as *Gowanus, Brooklyn* not only got into Sundance, it also won the coveted short film prize there which brought attention to the feature film script version that Fleck and Boden had already written. Further aiding them with the script development process was their acceptance to the Sundance Screenwriters Lab. Ultimately the feature film version of *Gowanus, Brooklyn* was made as *Half Nelson* and accepted into the Sundance Film Festival in 2006 where it found theatrical distribution from Think Film and Axiom Films. Although it wasn't a huge financial hit, it became a critical darling and ignited the careers of Ryan Fleck and Anna Boden. And Gosling.

It's Always Sunny in Philadelphia (2005–present)

This much loved television sitcom was based on an amateur short film that was made by Rob McElhenney, Glen Howerton, and Charlie Day who not only made the short, but also starred in it as well. The short film was called *Charlie Has Cancer* and according to *Fandom*, the short was made with two simple camcorders for an estimated cost of $85–$200 which was used almost solely to purchase the video tapes for the cameras.[11] Now in its twelfth season (and renewed for a thirteenth and fourteenth season as well), the short film jump-started the careers of its creators as both writers/producers and actors.

Napoleon Dynamite (2004)

While still a student at Brigham Young University in Utah, writer/director Jared Hess made a short film for a class assignment. It was a nine-minute short shot on black and white film over the course of two days for the total cost of $500. The short was called *Peluca* and it featured the actor Jon Heder in the same part that he later played in the feature film, *Napoleon Dynamite*. "Peluca" refers to the wig that is purchased in the film. The short was selected by the 2003 Slamdance Film Festival where it caught the interest of investors. From there Jared Hess wrote and directed the feature that became *Napoleon Dynamite*, which was then selected by the Sundance Film Festival in 2014 where the theatrical distribution rights were acquired by Fox Searchlight and Paramount Pictures, in association with MTV Films. And to think it all started with a class assignment!

Lock, Stock and Two Smoking Barrels (1998)

In 1995, Guy Ritchie wrote and directed the twenty-minute short film, *The Hard Case*. Trudie Styler, the wife of Sting, saw the movie and invested in what became the feature version titled, *Lock, Stock and Two Smoking Barrels*. The feature film not only launched his career, it also introduced him to Madonna, his future ex-wife, as the soundtrack for *Lock, Stock and Two Smoking Barrels* was issued on Madonna's Maverick Records. Guy Ritchie's career hasn't missed a beat as it now includes such films as the two Robert Downey, Jr., *Sherlock Holmes* movies and the soon to be released *King Arthur: Legend of the Sword*.[12] All that from a short film.

Boogie Nights (1997)

This award-winning film is based on the short film titled *The Dirk Diggler Story* (1987). When he was seventeen years old, Paul Thomas Anderson wrote and directed *The Dirk Diggler Story* in a mockumentary style about the rise and fall of a well-endowed male porn star. According to the Internet site Doom Rocket, Paul Thomas Anderson was obsessed with the movie *Spinal Tap* (a famous mockumentary about a fake British rock band) and it was from that movie that he conceived of the idea for *The Dirk Diggler Story* which later became *Boogie Nights* starring Mark Wahlberg.[13] What's especially interesting is how Paul Thomas Anderson had the habit of first creating other short films which then became the genesis for his longer feature films. Examples include *Hard 8* (1996), which was based on the short film *Cigarettes and Coffee* and *Punch Drunk Love* (2002), which was based on *Couch*.

Sling Blade (1996)

Billy Bob Thornton wrote and starred in both the feature film *Sling Blade* and the short film *Some Folks Call It A Sling Blade* on which the feature is based. The short film had a very healthy budget of $55,000 and was directed by George Hickenlooper, the Emmy-winning director of the documentary about the making of *Apocalypse Now*. But according to the *Los Angeles Times*, by the time the short film aired at the Sundance Film Festival in January of 1994, the star and director were no longer talking with each other as they disagreed over the editing of a key monologue. And Thornton said that the feature script was not based on the short but rather on a monologue from a one-man show, *Swine Before Pearls*, that he wrote and performed starting in 1986. Regardless, Thornton went on to write, direct, and star in *Sling Blade* for which he won the Academy Award for Best Adapted Screenplay as well as a nomination for Best Actor in a Leading Role.[14]

Bottle Rocket (1996)

This feature film is based on the black and white short film of the same name. Proving that a student's first contact or collaborator is often a college classmate, writer/director Wes Anderson and actor Luke Wilson shared a playwriting class at University of Texas in Austin. The short starred brothers Owen and Luke Wilson. While Wes Anderson's short film did get accepted into the 1992 Sundance Film Festival, it was not a big hit. However, it did catch the attention of producer James L. Brooks and launched the careers of writer/director Wes Anderson and actors Luke and Owen Wilson.

12 Monkeys (1995)

In 1962, French New Wave filmmaker Chris Marker made a twenty-eight-minute science fiction short film titled *Le Jetee* about a post-nuclear war experiment in time travel.[15] Many years later,

Universal Studios acquired the rights to make the short as a feature film which then became *12 Monkeys* and later a television series. Terry Gilliam directed and Bruce Willis, Madeleine Stowe, and Brad Pitt starred in it. Pitt won a Golden Globe for his performance and was nominated for the Academy Award for Best Supporting Actor.

THX 1138

Back in 1967, when he was at University of Southern California (USC) film school, George Lucas wrote and directed the student film, *Electronic Labyrinth: THX 1138 4EB* about a dystopian future. It was an ambitious film for a student work. At that time, USC had a working arrangement with the United States Navy wherein they were expected to teach Navy filmmakers, but it wasn't a class that most USC professors wanted to teach. So Lucas taught the class and used the Navy filmmakers as his crew and the Navy paid for all the color film stock and the lab processing costs. Because of his connection with the Navy, Lucas was given access to local airports and other locations that would have otherwise been off-limits. The short film won first prize at the third National Student Film Festival in 1968. Attending that festival were industry executives and Steven Spielberg.[16] A few years later, in 1971, Lucas turned the short film into the theatrical feature, *THX 1138,* which went on to launch his career. Most of us have never seen *THX 1138* but everyone has seen *Star Wars.*

In conclusion, we hope you have a better understanding of just how powerful your short film can be in terms of jump-starting and then moving your career forward. Whether you're looking for an opportunity to direct or even a way to find a Hollywood spouse, remember, it all starts with the short script.

ENDNOTES

1. https://en.wikipedia.org/wiki/Mean_Girls

2. http://www.imdb.com/title/tt2582802

3. https://en.wikipedia.org/wiki/Black_List_(survey)

4. http://www.imdb.com/title/tt3186318/plotsummary?ref_=tt_ov_pl

5. https://en.wikipedia.org/wiki/Jay_and_Seth_versus_the_Apocalypse

6. http://www.ew.com/article/2008/06/12/jay-seth-apocal

7. https://www.youtube.com/watch?v=WRqS6pBC42w

8. http://www.slate.com/blogs/browbeat/2012/10/05/frankenweenie_watch_the_original_1984_tim_burton_short_via_youtube_.html

9. http://www.premiumbeat.com/blog/8-great-proof-of-concept-films-that-got-picked-up-by-hollywood/

10. http://filmmakermagazine.com/archives/issues/summer2006/features/check_head.php#.V_acANxQJyc

11. http://itsalwayssunny.wikia.com/wiki/Charlie_Has_Cancer_(Original_Pilot)

12. https://en.wikipedia.org/wiki/Guy_Ritchie

13. http://doomrocket.com/uncultured-the-dirk-diggler-story/

14. http://articles.orlandosentinel.com/1997-04-06/entertainment/9704040790_1_sling-blade-thornton-george-hickenlooper

15. https://en.wikipedia.org/wiki/La_Jet%C3%A9e

16. https://en.wikipedia.org/wiki/Electronic_Labyrinth:_THX_1138_4EB

SHORT FILM, LONG CAREER

Writing an excellent proof of concept short film requires a good story that has well developed characters, lots of turning points in the plot, a solid theme and a surprise zinger ending. But in a purely practical sense, a proof of concept short film must be something that you can actually film.

LIST LOCATIONS TO WHICH YOU HAVE ACCESS FOR FILMING.

1

2

3

4

LIST INTERESTING PROPS IN YOUR HOME OR DORM ROOM THAT COULD BE USED IN A SHORT FILM.

1

2

3

4

LIST ACTORS THAT YOU KNOW. IF YOU DON'T KNOW ANY, LIST SITES WHERE YOU COULD ADVERTISE FOR ACTORS.

1

2

3

4

CHAPTER

All in the Cards

CARDING OUT THE 100-PAGE SCREENPLAY

Let's face it. There is no money in short films. We doubt anyone has ever put down on their tax return: SHORT FILM WRITER as occupation. The goal of writing a short film is that it leads to something bigger, better, and more lucrative. It is also a great way of learning what it takes to write a screenplay or television pilot. The same dramatic tenets appear in both.

We are going to talk about long-form structure as it applies to feature film writing. We do put in television examples also because the basics of all drama apply to every written form of modern entertainment.

Everything old is new again. Podcasts like *Welcome to Nightvale* follow a dramatic structure similar to film and television. Video games like *The Last of Us* are structured like feature films.

The "Classic" Three-Act Structure

Everything has a beginning, middle, and an end. There's Act One, Act Two, Act Three. These are terms taken from the theater. Act One implies the curtain going up. The end of Act Three, it goes down. You're writing without the curtains.

In a one hundred-page script, Act One would be about twenty-five pages, Act Two about fifty pages, Act Three another twenty-five. There's a balance. Most books we have read repeat the same information with minor variations.

Why one hundred pages?

For the new writer, you should be writing something that is character driven. High concept, low budget. Something that is a quick read but that can be produced maybe by your own team.

- ▶ *Safety Not Guaranteed* by Derek Connolly clocked in at ninety-seven pages. It was directed by Colin Trevorrow. Connolly would go on to write *Jurassic World* and *Kong: Skull Island.*
- ▶ *Whiplash* by Damien Chazelle was 111 pages long, but very self-contained in terms of character and location. Chazelle directed the film. *La La Land* came in at ninety-six pages.
- ▶ *Bright* by Max Landis was under one hundred pages. It sold for a reported $3 million to Netflix as a movie.

Again, there are never forced page counts. Scripts vary from 100–150 pages. Look at the longer scripts for *12 Years a Slave* or *The Social Network*. But those are by established writers. When looking for ways to break in:

- ▶ Write something that shows you have a command of the form.
- ▶ Write something that has a chance to get produced.
- ▶ Write something that is character-driven.

Long-Form Structure Screenplay

Here is one way to simplify structure in terms of punctuation.

Act One ends with a ? (question mark). We wonder what is going to happen. Is the protagonist going to achieve their goal?

Act Two ends with an ! (exclamation point). It's the "Oh No!" moment where all seems lost. Or where the protagonist now has a new goal or stands at the edge of a new battle.

Act Three ends with a . (period). There's a finality to the story. It's over.

We divide Act Two into two acts. Act Two-A and Act Two-B. The divide is at the MIDPOINT of the story. The midpoint is treated like a curtain coming down at the intermission of a Broadway show. So in some ways Hollywood is working in a four-act structure. But no one will ever say that.

The midpoint is like another act break. And it's also balanced. So a one hundred-page script's Act Two would be divided into a twenty-five-page Act Two-A and a twenty-five-page Act Two-B.

For television, the pilot episode is basically Act One of the series. Act Two might run seven seasons. Act Three is the last episode, or the last season.

THE MINI-MOVIE APPROACH

It's very hard to write a feature-length script. But can you write a thirteen-page script? Sure. I can do that, you think. Well, that's what we're going to do. We're going to write eight mini-movies. Each one thirteen pages long.

We're going to break them down into EIGHT MINI-MOVIES or EIGHT SEQUENCES.

Each sequence is different. Think of the sequences like movements in a symphony. There are different movements, different pacing of the composition where the main theme repeats and reemerges, carried by different sections of the orchestra, just as the themes of a movie are carried by different characters. It crescendos at the end and has a rousing conclusion.

The mini-movie approach is a way to keep your story moving; to keep it interesting. The mini-movie approach has been around for years. Hitchcock used it: think about a movie like *North by Northwest* (If you haven't seen it, please put it on top of your rental list). There's the *Crop Duster* mini-movie, there's the *Flight on Lincoln's Nose* mini-movie, and there's the great *Seduction on the Train* mini-movie with Cary and Eva Marie Saint. These are sequences within the whole movie.

Now within each of these mini-movies are SEQUENCES and SCENES. We want to go through an overview of the mini-movie approach.

ACT ONE		ACT TWO-A		ACT TWO-B		ACT THREE	
Pages 1–25		Pages 25–50		Pages 50–75		Pages 75–100	
THE SET-UP		CONFLICT AND CONFRONTATION		DEVELOPMENT AND CRISIS		RESOLUTION	
Sequence 1– Opening	Sequence 2–Set-Up	Sequence 3– The New World	Sequence 4– Midpoint	Sequence 5– Development	Sequence 6– Crisis	Sequence 7– Last Great Decision	Sequence 8– Battle/ Resolution

Sequence 1—The Opening

The first pages of your script equals the first twelve to fifteen minutes of a movie. It's the who, what, when, and where part of the story. We are introduced to the life of the protagonist. We learn what the TONE of the movie is going to be. Comedy? Drama? Sci-fi? This little movie is showing us what the protagonist's life is like if the rest of the movie doesn't happen. We get some exposition. This is the part where the audience has the most patience. However, know this—you get about thirteen pages to draw the reader in. That's it. If you don't establish a great character that we can relate to in that first sequence, it's going to be a hard sell. At the end of the sequence, something happens. It's what disrupts the protagonist's life. It's called the Inciting Incident. The renowned mythologist Joseph Campbell called it the Call to Adventure in his book *The Hero With a Thousand Faces*. It starts the protagonist on their journey. It's something the protagonist is going to have to deal with. Unlike a short film, it's NOT the end of the first act. It's a smaller event that sets the story into motion.

Sequence 2—The Set-Up

The next twelve to thirteen pages deal with the main character reacting to the inciting incident. We are still setting up the story. We are learning what the movie is going to be about. At the end of this sequence is the big END OF ACT ONE. Something completely disrupts the main character's life. The OBJECTIVE is established and we have introduced the DRAMATIC QUESTION of the story.

ACT TWO-A

Sequence 3—The New World

The bulk of Act Two (usually) deals with the protagonist wanting to restore their life back to the way it was. The main DRAMATIC QUESTION has been introduced. Frodo has to get the ring to Mordor. Remember this—your protagonist is just like you. When faced with a problem, a human being will always try the easiest possible solution to the problem. In the Tom Cruise movie, *Jerry Maguire,* the titular character is fired at the end of Act One. He is going to start his own agency. He needs to get college star Cushman as his client. Although the movie as a whole has an overall goal, each sequence has its own goal. Mini-movies = mini-goals. So in this sequence Jerry's goal will be to get Cushman as a client. It all revolves around that! Nothing more. The protagonist is living in the moment, worried about the task at hand. In the *Lord of the Rings: The Fellowship of the Ring,* Frodo has to go to the inn and meet Gandalf. That is his goal. At the end of this sequence, something happens which spins the story into the next sequence. Jerry Maguire achieves his goal—he gets Cushman. This leads to the next sequence. Frodo gets to the inn and there is no Gandalf. There is only Aragorn who agrees to help and they head off to the next place and sequence.

Sequence 4—The Midpoint/ Major Character Shift

The protagonist is still trying to fix the problem. Jerry Maguire is looking to get back on top as an agent. So what happens? He gets Cushman as a client but he wants to be first in the NFL draft. We see the NFL draft, a great sequence in the hotel which builds and builds, and we see that Jerry loses Cushman and his girlfriend. That is the MIDPOINT. The midpoint of the movie is a very important beat. It divides the story in half. Usually there's a <u>major character shift.</u> Remember: all your protagonist wants to do is restore his or her life to the status quo. This is where they learn it's going to be harder than they thought. Here's a little something to think about: the midpoint of the movie usually points to the end of the movie. This is why it is so important for you to know the ending of your story. At the end of *Shrek,* Shrek married Fiona. At the midpoint is where ogre and ogre meet, face-to-face. At the end of *The Godfather,* Michael takes over the crime syndicate. At the midpoint, he commits murder for the family. In *The Hunger Games,* the games begin at the midpoint and Katniss has to fight for her life. By the end, Katniss is a winner of the games.

ACT TWO-B

Sequence 5—Development

The last two sequences dealt with mini-goals. Now what happens is a little different. The movie slows down. This is the sequence where the theme starts to come forward. This is the reason you wrote the movie. Think of the movie *Witness.* What scene comes to mind? I'm betting it's building the barn.

Now, think about this. That scene has absolutely nothing to do with solving the plot of the story. *Witness* is about John Book trying to catch the bad cops. But what it's really about are two people from different worlds falling in love. John Book is not going toward his goal. This part of the story had nothing to do with the movie and IT HAS EVERYTHING TO DO WITH THE MOVIE. It's the reason the movie is good. It's the reason the movie was written. In *Shrek,* this is where Shrek and Fiona are falling in love. In *The Godfather,* it's where Michael is walking around Sicily and getting married. Then finally at the end of the sequence, something jolts the protagonist back into the story.

Sequence 6—Crisis

Now it's getting bad for the protagonist. We are getting to the end of the second act. Later we will talk about what types of end of Act Two's there are, but for now think of it like this: when you get to the end of Act Two, your protagonist is at a crisis point. It looks really bad for the protagonist. It looks like they are not going to be able to achieve the goal. It seems all is going to be lost.

ACT THREE

Sequence 7—The Last Great Decision

The protagonist goes into the last act feeling pretty bad. In this sequence they are faced with a decision which ends at the conclusion of this sequence. Do I go back to the person I was before or do I become a new, better person? In *Shrek,* all the ogre wants is his swamp back and to be left alone. Well, he has achieved his goal. He has his swamp. Problem: he now loves the girl. What does he do? He chooses to fight.

Sequence 8—Resolution

Finally, we get to the final battle. The protagonist fights their last fight and emerges a much different, smarter person than they were in the beginning. The pole-to-pole transformation is complete. Rose in *Titanic* has gone from a privileged rich young woman to someone who is going to live her own life and achieve her own destiny.

Building the Board

We believe the new feature writer should be crafting a one hundred-page screenplay. Most screenwriters still use index cards to card out their story. Simple blank index cards pinned to a corkboard help to visualize the story. This has been our approach professionally in Hollywood and in the classroom.

We want to take a moment to emphasize that the forty cards we are going to suggest are not etched in stone. There is no paradigm that matches every movie. But there are dramatic motifs that have appeared and continue to appear consistently from the beginning days of drama. We don't tell you to put a Dark Night of the Hero Who is Lost with his Cat moment on page twenty-three.

Visualizing a story with index cards on a board helps writers see their movie or television series before they start writing. These boards are all over the walls of the writers' room of television shows. They fill the halls of Disney and Pixar.

Let's see your movie before you write it. We list the forty CARDS we use below in the chart and define each one after that.

ACT ONE		ACT TWO-A		ACT TWO-B		ACT THREE	
Pages 1–25		Pages 25–50		Pages 50–75		Pages 75–100	
THE SET-UP		CONFLICT AND CONFRONTATION		DEVELOPMENT AND CRISIS		RESOLUTION	
Sequence 1–Opening	Sequence 2–Set-Up	Sequence 3–The New World	Sequence 4–Midpoint	Sequence 5–Development	Sequence 6–Crisis	Sequence 7–Last Great Decision	Sequence 8–Battle/Resolution
Open with a Hook	Refusal of the Call	Enter the New World	Second Attempt	Reaction to the Midpoint	A Final Push	The Big Gloom	Battle
Defining Action	Meeting with the Mentor	Initial Goal	Hope and Fear	Develop Theme	Rewards/Setbacks	Who am I?	Convergence
Status Quo/Pole-to-Pole Transformation	Dramatic Question	New Rules/New Appearances	Track the Subplots	Not Just about the Hero Anymore	Expose the Character's Weakness	Help from the Mentor	Resurrection/Sacrifice
Exposition	Thematic Question	Promise of the Premise	Ramping Up	Intimacy Through Failure	Calm Before the Storm	Ticking Clock	Magic Flight/Chase
Inciting Incident	Protagonist and Objective	First Attempt Fails or Not	Midpoint/Major Character Shift	The Unexpected	End of Act Two	Last Great Decision	Return with the Elixir/The New Me

The bottom row of cards is the foundation. It holds the structure together.

Each sequence has a beginning, middle, and end.

The bottom cards are the end of the sequence and contain the TURNING POINTS.

The TURNING POINTS spin the story in a new direction.

THE CARDS

Open with a Hook

The opening image, the first scene of your movie, needs to draw the audience in. Avoid opening with talking heads. Stories tend to open with something already in motion.

> *La La Land*—opens with Los Angelenos stuck in traffic and breaking into song.
>
> *Breaking Bad*—Walt is in a gas mask. He has a gun. Jessie is passed out. People are dead. Walt records a message to his wife and family. Sirens are heard approaching.

Defining Action

A character is quickly defined by what they are doing when we meet them. You want to establish the status quo of the movie.

> *The Force Awakens*—Finn is the reluctant storm trooper. He can't kill. He shows compassion. He runs away. Poe is a cocky fighter pilot not afraid to trade barbs with Kylo Ren.
>
> *How to Get Away with Murder*—Annalise Keating is the no-nonsense lawyer/professor who commands the lecture room.

Status Quo—Pole-to-Pole Transformation

You want to show us what the character's life would be like if the movie had never taken place. Who your characters are in the beginning is as important as who they become at the end. This is why stories start slow and end fast. You need to set up the world of the story. We need to see Dorothy in Kansas in black and white before she goes off to Oz. Think about POLE-TO-POLE TRANSFORMATION. You need to know who and what your character is at the END of the movie.

> *Don't Think Twice*—the improv group is a family. They perform and bond together. By the end of the movie, they are still friends but the group has broken up and all have moved on to different lives.
>
> *Stranger Things*—the young friends are playing Dungeons and Dragons in the basement. By the end of the first season, they have lived dungeons and dragons.

Exposition

You are now telling us only what we need to know at this point. What is important to establishing the status quo of the hero at this point in time? You have started to establish the "who" of the story. Now you need to show us the what, when, where, and why.

> *Green Room*—the punk rock band is struggling for cash, driving around the Northwest and loses another gig.
>
> *House of Cards*—Frank Underwood despises everyone around him and has the magic of manipulation. We are in the world of Washington D.C. politics.

Inciting Incident

Something is introduced into the story which upsets the status quo of the story. From here on the hero will react to this event. TIP: the main character does not know the severity of the inciting incident but the audience should be aware that something is brewing. For example, in an action movie like *Die Hard*, the audience is aware of the robbery in progress before the hero.

> *Deadpool*—Wade Wilson learns he has cancer and is going to die. Suddenly his entire life has changed. He doesn't become Deadpool yet. That happens later in Act One. But that can't happen unless this inciting incident occurs.
>
> *Battlestar Galactica*—humanity is attacked by the Cylons. This kicks the story into motion.

Refusal of the Call

The hero or someone close to the hero will express a reluctance; a fear that this is not a good idea. Don't be afraid to have your characters react to what is happening to them. Fears and concerns are emotions we all share. You want to make your protagonist human.

> *Green Room*—the band has played for the Neo-Nazis and has witnessed a murder. They are asked to wait in the green room until the police arrive. Here they react to their situation. They can't believe this is happening.
>
> *Neighbors*—Mac and Kelly can't believe they now live next door to a frat house.

Meeting with the Mentor

The hero will usually meet a mentor. A friend. Someone who is going to be their guide on the journey. TIP: a mentor can be a best friend. A boss. A teacher. Sometimes it is the sidekick character. This is the wise soul. The mentor is the conscious of the movie. Do not forget to introduce the ANTAGONIST.

> *Whiplash*—Fletcher is the antagonist to Andrew but he is also his mentor. Andrew's father is featured more prominently in the script as a "mentor."
>
> *Creed*—Rocky is the mentor for Adonis. In a nice dramatic touch, Ryan Coogler (writer/director) allows Rocky to learn from his old mentor's son.

Dramatic Question

The page seventeen rule. Yes, there is one rule. The next time you are watching a movie, check your watch. Something usually happens around seventeen minutes into a movie which will tell us what the movie is going to be about. This is not the end of the first act. This is where you tell the audience what the movie is really going to be about. It's when Indiana Jones and the audience learn what the Lost Ark is.

Deadpool—Wade Wilson is experimented upon which causes him to have superpowers.
The Martian—Mark Watney lays out his plan on how to survive. It's not the end of the first act. That is the big turn when NASA realizes he might still be alive.

Thematic Question

At some point, you need to tell us what and why you are writing. Don't be afraid to have a character SAY what the movie is about out loud. It might not be the right time here to express the theme but it should be hinted at in the first act.

The Fast and the Furious—pretty much any one of this franchise has the creed of: I don't have friends, I have family. They are a unit.
Straight Outta Compton—our story needs to be told by any voice necessary.

Protagonist and Objective

The hero begins his/her journey. They are now heading toward a new world and/or a new goal. Their lives have been disrupted and this is the only chance they have to return it to the status quo that was established in Act One. YOU CAN NOT CONTINUE UNTIL YOU KNOW WHAT YOUR MAIN CHARACTER WANTS!

Mad Max: Fury Road—even though it is called Mad Max, it might as well have been called Mad Furiosa. Imperator Furiosa wants to lead the young women and escape to safety. Max has the same objective to escape.
Finding Dory—Dory wants to find her family and sets out to do so.

ACT TWO-A

The New World

The hero enters a new world. A different place than they were before. This place can be the beginning of a relationship, a new romance, a physical transformation to a new location.

> *Back to the Future*—a classic. Marty McFly enters the world of his hometown in 1955.
> *Spy*—Susan Cooper enters the world of being a spy.

Initial Goal

A character, like a person, will take the easiest course of action to solve their problem. That will either fail or succeed but spin into a larger problem. This sequence is about taking that easy first step.

> *Back to the Future*—Marty's initial goal is to find Doc Brown and figure out how to get back to his time.
> *The Martian*—Mark Watney needs to grow potatoes. A pretty simple goal for a very high concept movie.

New Rules, New Appearances

A hero needs to learn the new rules and often will take a disguise, in terms of a hidden change of attitude. When you come to a new country, you have to abide by the rules.

> *Orange is the New Black*—Piper has to learn the rules of prison life.
> *Mike and Dave Need Wedding Dates*—they need dates but their dates are pretending to be a lot sweeter than the party girls they are.

Promise of the Premise

The writer needs to deliver what they promised in the premise of the story. This needs to happen in every act. This is one of those cards that reminds the writer to have the extended comedic set piece or car chase.

> *Skyfall*—every sequence features action set pieces. Joel Silver, producer of the *Die Hard* movies, used to say that every script needs to deliver a "whammo" to the audience every ten pages.
> *The Girl on the Train*—delivers the mystery. It keeps giving up clues as the audience leans in and wonders who really did what to whom.

First Attempt Fails or Not

Remember that initial goal of the sequence. This is the moment where we see if the protagonist achieves that goal or has to try something new. Often, it is a fail.

The Forty Year Old Virgin—Andy's overall objective was to lose his virginity. His initial goal thrust upon him by his friend was to seal the deal with a very drunk woman in a bar. Andy's attempt ended with him almost dying in a car crash and his date vomiting all over him. A fail.

World War Z—Gerry Lane is trying to find the cure for the zombie infection. His initial goal took him to South Korea to find a doctor who might have a cure. They are ambushed, almost killed by the zombies, and the doctor has killed himself. A fail.

Second Attempt

The protagonist now has to regroup and come up with another plan. Or if the movie is an extended journey, this "second attempt" could be another location. Road movies tend to be like this.

Finding Nemo is a road movie as Marlin searches for Nemo. The sequences are: encounter with Bruce the Shark, the jellyfish, the Gulf Stream, the drainage pipes.

Star Wars: The Force Awakens—having escaped, Rey and Finn find Han Solo and Chewbacca. After a fun "promise of the premise" scene where they escape outlaws and aliens, the crew travels to the planet Takodana and meets with cantina owner, Maz Kanata.

Wall-E—the love-struck robot has to find Eve.

Hope and Fear

This is another of those cards that is a reminder card. All movies are hope and fear. You should always be hoping for one thing to happen to the heroes and fear that it will not.

Room—you hope and pray Ma and Jack will get out of the room and escape but fear they won't. Then later you hope they can adjust to life outside and fear they won't.

Titanic—you hope Jack and Rose will survive and live happily ever after. But you fear they won't.

Track the Subplots

Subplots are the "B" stories that sometimes carry the theme of the main story. They might be the romance under the main plot. Subplots ask their own dramatic questions. They are the stories under the stories. Television calls the subplots the B and C stories.

Ocean's 11—Danny Ocean is robbing a casino. But the subplot is: will Danny get his wife Tess back?

Ex-Machina—the main plot is Caleb psychologically testing Ava, but the subplot is when he starts to fall in love with her.

Ramping Up

You should think of this scene as a preparation scene or a scene of anticipation. And it does usually happen before the midpoint of the movie. The dramatic purpose to prep the audience for something big that is coming up; something that will shift the character.

> *Star Wars: The Force Awakens*—this is where we arrive at Takodana and meet with cantina owner, Maz Kanata. The audience learns that the First Order is on their way and knows the location of our heroes. Maz is intrigued by Rey.
>
> *Shrek*—Shrek and Donkey approach the castle. They have to cross a drawbridge over a molten river and survive a dragon as they attempt to rescue Fiona.

Midpoint/Major Character Shift

This is the act break that occurs at the end of Two-A and leads to Two-B. What is significant is that a major character shift is going to occur. A romance might begin. Also, the midpoint is an event which the hero approaches with some trepidation. It's a location, an event that the audience is anticipating. An overly simple but sometimes effective way of looking at the midpoint is that it divides Act Two into two halves. So if good things were happening in the first half of Act Two, then bad things happen in the next part of Act Two. Also, the midpoint points to the ending of the movie.

> *Lord of the Rings: Fellowship of the Ring*—the factions are together, but not united. They argue about how to handle the ring. It is Frodo who steps up and declares he will do it. This unites them and forms the fellowship. It is also a major character change for Frodo as he now has unknowingly become the leader.
>
> *Trainwreck*—Aaron wants to be in a relationship with Amy. He might as well be speaking a different language. She is not prepared for this but gives it a try. For this movie and this character, this is a major shift which hints at the ending of the story.

ACT TWO-B

Reaction to the Midpoint

A character will always react to what has just happened. It doesn't have to happen immediately, but remember, we are looking to see characters making choices in crisis which leads to change. We want to see them be emotional.

> *The Social Network*—at the midpoint, Sean Parker has shown up. He wants to help. He sees a larger vision for Facebook. Mark and Eduardo disagree about Sean's involvement.
>
> *Juno*—Juno is taken with Mark. Juno's boyfriend and mother argue with her about the direction her life has taken and her interest in a married man.

Develop Theme

Another card that is a reminder. Theme should be prevalent throughout the script. You need to be writing about something. You should have something to say about the human condition. The theme has been informing the story throughout.

The Dark Knight Returns—The Joker expresses the theme: "Desperation causes men to act in self-destructive and chaotic ways." The Joker can be talking about himself, or he might be talking about what he is trying to make Bruce Wayne/Batman do and become.

Black Swan—the theme that artistic expression can lead to madness is one of the many themes expressed. It is enhanced through the visuals and through the dialogue. It's the battle of the Black Swan and White Swan and is stated in the script: "But which of you can embody both swans?"

Not Just about the Hero Anymore

As the second act progresses, the protagonist will have more to lose if they fail to achieve their goal. There is more at stake. There are more characters involved. Relationships have developed.

The Guardians of the Galaxy—not just about Starlord and searching for treasure. It's about Starlord and his friends now having to save the universe.

Up—Carl just wanted to be left alone. Now he has a kid and a dog to worry about.

Intimacy through Failure

We like to watch the hero fail. How they react to adversity is how we learn from them; how we empathize with them. We want to see how a character deals with failure. We want to learn from the story. Movies are usually about someone wanting something and they are having a hard time getting it.

The Hangover—the three hapless heroes continue to get plummeted every time they think they are getting closer to finding Doug. They are shot at, abused by the police, and have to survive Mike Tyson and his tiger. With comedies, it keeps getting worse.

Avatar—Jake can't stop the Tree of Life from being destroyed. He watches his mentor die. Each of these scenes bonds us more to the character.

The Unexpected

Often an event will jolt the story back into the narrative. Something will happen to push the protagonists toward the end of the second act.

Cast Away—Chuck Nolan has failed. He believes he will die on the island when a piece of the wreckage washes on shore. He looks at it and turns it into a sail.

Finding Nemo—as he hangs on for life in the mouth of a whale, Marlin realizes he has to let go. Not just to survive the whale but to be a better father. It's theme and action coming together.

A Final Push

The last sequence of the second act is beginning and the protagonist attempts to solve the problem that has only worsened since the beginning of Act Two.

The Devil Wears Prada—Andie Sachs is determined not to give in to Miranda, to take whatever the woman can dish out.

The Arrival—Linguist Dr. Louise Baker has to make a furious effort to communicate with the aliens before a war begins.

Rewards/Setbacks

For the protagonist, there are always going to be rewards and setbacks.

10 Cloverfield Lane—Michelle, worried for her and Emmet's safety, has been gathering material to make a biohazard suit to escape the bunker. She has successfully assembled the suit (rewards) but then Howard finds out (setback).

Forrest Gump—Forrest has become rich. He finds Jenny. Marries her. Later, he learns he has a son. Forrest endures many rewards and setbacks—sometimes from scene to scene. It can be a good balance.

Expose the Character Weakness

At some point, the hero will reveal or we will see a side of the hero we haven't before. Sometimes it is what haunts the hero.

Inception—Cobb is still living in fear of Mal. His backstory is revealed. As written on Wikia: "During an experiment in Dream-Sharing, Dom insisted on going deeper into the different layers of dreams. This resulted in the two becoming trapped in Limbo, unconstructed dream space. The two spent around fifty years building a city around them, with many buildings created from memories of their past."[1] Basically, in a very complex manner, we learn what has haunted Cobb.

Shrek—Fiona is revealed to be an ogre. A lot simpler than *Inception* but just as effective.

Calm before the Storm

Often a story will come to a halt just before the proverbial stuff hits the fan. Characters might express worry, or optimism appears only to have it all fall apart a few minutes later.

> *Wedding Crashers*—John has fallen in love with Claire, and he might actually tell her the truth about his wedding crashing lies. But then the end of the second act occurs…
>
> *Jaws*—a classic. Brody, Quint, and Hooper sit on the boat, drinking and comparing scars. This leads to the iconic Quint (Robert Shaw) monologue about why he is afraid of sharks. As he tells the tale of how he survived the sinking of the U.S.S. Indianapolis, we are moments from the last act. Also this scene effectively combines EXPOSING THE CHARCTER WEAKNESS with the calm. The cards are there as markers, reminders. Move them around. Combine them. But hit the beats.

END OF ACT TWO

The hero encounters a huge setback or the story takes an unexpected turn, pushing us into the last act. In the punctuation of structure, this act ends with a huge exclamation point (!). Something major has happened. The hero is at an emotional crossroads. Sometimes their original goal has been met, but over the course of the story the goal has changed. Movies are about heroes not getting what they want but sometimes getting what they need. The end of Act Two can be bad things happen, a new goal, or edge of battle.

> *E.T. The Extra Terrestrial*—E.T. is captured. Elliot is sick and E.T. might not get home.
>
> *Saving Private Ryan*—Ryan refuses to leave his post forcing Miller and his team to join the final battle.

ACT THREE

The Big Gloom

As the third act begins, the protagonist is again reacting to what has just happened. They are feeling bad and the writer cannot be afraid to show it. They think they have failed.

> *Shrek*—Shrek sits alone as he sends Fiona off to get married to the king.
>
> *Gravity*—after a last ditch attempt at radio communication with an Eskimo–Aleut-speaking fisherman on Earth, Stone realizes she is going to be stranded. She shuts down the cabin's oxygen supply to commit suicide.

Who Am I?

Characters now are having their identity crisis. They don't know who they are—emotionally. Do they want to be the person they were at the start of story, or do they evolve?

Up in the Air—Ryan Bingham is a man who has travelled a million miles in the air, attended his sister's wedding, and is not sure what he wants anymore: to be alone or to be with the woman he loves.

The Departed—Billy is the cop undercover as the mobster. Colin is the mobster who is the undercover cop. They are both in love with Madolyn and have no idea of who they are anymore.

Help from the Mentor

Sometimes the hero needs a push from a friend. Someone who can help them achieve their goal. It doesn't make the main character weak. It makes them human. It's the friend who is not scared to tell you how stupid you are.

Forgetting Sarah Marshall—Bill Hader plays Brian, Peter's best friend. Throughout the movie, Brian has been giving advice on what Peter needs to do. In *Trainwreck*, Bill Hader is now the romantic lead getting advice from his patient, LeBron James.

Skyfall—M and Bond are in the shootout against Silva. M has been his mentor for years. Now she is by his side as the final battle converges at Skyfall, Bond's childhood home.

Ticking Clock

If you have not set up the timer on the Death Star, now is the time. Stories tend to accelerate toward the end.

Inception—Cobb and his team are "incepting" on three levels. Three stories are going on at once. If they can't get out in time, they will be lost forever. If they can't incept the idea in time, their plan fails.

The Hunger Games—the ticking clock is the other participants. As they are killed off, Katniss knows she is running out of time.

Last Great Decision

The hero has a choice to go back to be the person they were in the beginning of the movie or to change. Remember, characters are reluctant to change. It's the last thing they want to do.

Million Dollar Baby—Maggie is paralyzed. All she ever wanted to do was fight. Now she makes the decision and she wants to die. She wants Frankie to help her.

127 Hours—Aron Ralston has been trapped under a boulder since the end of Act One. Now as he has relived his life in his mind he faces a life or death decision. To live, he has to saw his own arm off.

Battle

There will be a final battle. This is where the forces of antagonism come face-to-face with the protagonist. It can be on the rooftops of Gotham, in a living room—as long as they are finally mano a mano in the last moments of the movie.

Flight—the final trial is the final battle in this drama. It has a nice twist as Whip Whitaker, the man who saved lives, admits he was high and drinking.

Elf—Elf saves Santa Clause and fights the Central Park Rangers on Christmas Eve in Central Park.

Convergence

At this point, all the characters should be converging to the same time and space. You are wrapping up all the subplots. What is special about the location where the final battle is taking place?

Chinatown—There is a reason the classic movie is called *Chinatown* as that is where the back-story takes us; it's where Gitte's "ghost" resides.

Neighbors—Frat house craziness is how this comedy must end. Police. Fireworks. Neighbors vs. neighbors.

Resurrection/Sacrifice

There will/should be an apparent defeat. The hero is at the brink of death and then brought back. A relationship which was seemingly over now comes back to life. The hero gives up something, showing us how much they have changed. It might happen earlier but it does need to happen.

The Matrix—Neo appears to have died and we see his resurrection as he evolves into the One.

Titanic—Jack dies making sure Rose survives on the raft (Yes, that is what happened). He makes a sacrifice. We also see the present-day Rose die in her sleep. But then in her mind's eyes, we see the resurrection of their love in a sweeping shot on the Titanic. Rose and Jack are always together.

Magic Flight/Chase

Comedies have the race to the airport. Action movies have the race at the airport as planes are taking off and landing.

> *Fast and Furious 7*—a giant action scene where cars are chasing planes.
> *When Harry Met Sally*—Harry runs across town to get to Sally on New Year's Eve. (It's also convergence as it was the same place they were one year before.)

Return with the Elixir/the New Me

Finally in the last scene, you need to show us what the hero has gotten by going on this journey with you, the writer. What does the audience get? Great endings don't need to be happy endings. They just need to satisfy what has been set up.

> *10 Cloverfield Lane*—Michelle is no longer someone who runs from a fight. Now she turns the car around and heads to where the battle is. The earth is still under attack but it's an upbeat ending.
> *Star Wars: The Force Awakens*—Rey and Chewbacca find Luke Skywalker. Rey holds out the lightsaber. The audience goes crazy.

ENDNOTE

1. http://inception.wikia.com/wiki/Dominick_Cobb

break down a feature

CHAPTER 13

Short Films to Watch

The following short films are all on YouTube or Vimeo. They are listed in alphabetical order. We've selected them for their compelling story structure, evocative themes, memorable dialogue, and surprise zinger endings. They are also short films that we have watched multiple times and they have never failed to surprise or bore us.

SHORT FILMS: WATCH AND LEARN

Black Hole (2008); two minutes

> Winner of Virgin Media Shorts competition 2008, Best Filminute Award 2009, Gold Prize at the Smalls Award 2009, Winner Laugh Out Loud Festival 2012, Official Selection Cannes Court Metrage 2009.

> Written and directed by British filmmakers Philip Sansom and Olly Williams, *Black Hole* tells the story of an exhausted office worker who is working alone in a copy room one night only to discover a magical "black hole" that allows him to steal not only candy bars but stacks of cash. And like any good short film, the provocative ending is a cautionary tale. It's also exemplary for its strong visual storytelling.

Broken Night (2013); nine minutes

> Official Selection for 2013 Sundance Film Festival Shorts Competition.

> Written and directed by seasoned screenwriter Guillermo Arriaga, *Amores Perros, 21 Grams,* and *Babeland, Broken Night* was shot by Steven Spielberg's cinematographer and scored by Philip Glass. *Broken Night* tells the story of a mother and her daughter who are out driving in a remote west coast location when an accident causes things to go terribly wrong. Yes, it's a slick, moody film but it's an excellent short to view for its plants and payoffs. And the zinger, surprise ending does not disappoint.

Consent (2004); six minutes

Before his feature films *Juno, Up in the Air, Thank You For Smoking,* and *Young Adult,* Jason Reitman went to film school where he wrote and directed *Consent,* based on an idea by Michele Lee. *Consent* tells the story of a college couple who are about to hook up when they pause for a moment so they can clarify a few details about their potential sexual relationship. It's a great film to watch for the constant twists and turns in the plot. And the zinger ending adds a final twist to this comedic tale.

Curfew (2012); nineteen minutes

Winner of over forty-one awards including 2012 Academy Award for Best Live Action Short Film and presented at over eighty film festivals including the 2012 Tribeca Film Festival.[1] Actor Shawn Christensen wrote, directed, and starred in *Curfew* which tells the story of a drug addict who gets a call from his estranged sister to babysit his nine-year-old niece. What's particularly compelling about this short is not only the exemplary plotting but also the powerful emotional themes that it elicits.

Doodlebug (1997); three minutes

This student short film was written and directed by Christopher Nolan when he was still at University College London, long before he directed *Memento, Inception,* or the Batman trilogy of *Batman Begins, The Dark Knight,* and *The Dark Knight Rises. Doodlebug* is a psychological thriller about a man trying to kill a bug, only to discover that it's something far more profound than a bug. The zinger ending grabs us by surprise and the movie quickly ends. Nolan is known for his "brain benders"[2] in *Inception* and *Memento,* and it's striking to see similarities in this early work.

Eater (2007); eighteen minutes

Before brothers Matt and Ross Duffer created the recent Netflix hit, *Stranger Things,* they wrote and directed this creepy short about a rookie cop who works the night shift at a police station with a cannibal prisoner on the loose.[3] *Eater* is based on Peter Crowther's short story of the same name. The scary genius of the Duffer brothers is clearly evident in this deftly plotted horror flick that doesn't hold back. The zinger ending is chilling.

Floating (2014); nine minutes

Selected as a Vimeo Staff Pick in 2014.

Written and directed by Greg Jardin and co-written by Matthew Beans, *Floating* is a bittersweet movie about a being made up of balloons who wanders Los Angeles searching for connection. The entire story is told visually. Even without dialogue or a human face, we are granted access to the balloon's feelings and find ourselves tearing up in this emotionally powerful film.

God Of Love (2010); eighteen minutes

Winner of 2011 Academy Award for Best Live Action Short Film, 2010 Student Academy Awards, Special Jury Award at 2010 Aspen Shortsfest, Best Short Film at Heartland Film Festival, Christopher and Dana Reeve Award at Williamstown Film Festival, Best Student Short at 2010 Woodstock Film Festival.[4]

Written and directed by Luke Matheny, *God of Love* was his NYU Graduate thesis film and is best summarized by IMDb as, "A lovestruck, lounge-singing darts champion finds his prayers are answered—literally—when he mysteriously receives a box of love-inducing darts."[5] *God of Love* is an excellent example of how to structure a short film. From the opening hook to the inciting incident, midpoint—the end of Act Two—it hits every beat and tells a funny, quirky story.

Gridlock (2001); seven minutes

Nominated for 2003 Academy Award Best Live Action Short Film. Winner of 2002 Jury Award of Best Short Short at Aspen Shortsfest and awards at five other film festivals including Ghent, St. Louis, Sweden, Valladolid, and Woodstock.[6]

Written by Johan Verschueren and directed by Dirk Belien, *Gridlock*, is a Dutch short film about an irritated businessman who is stuck in traffic on a winter evening and when he uses a new cell phone for the first time to call his wife, dire consequences ensue. *Gridlock* has amazing twists and turns in its plotting and has probably one of the best surprise zinger endings in a short film.

Gulp (2001); seven minutes

Before he made the short film *Consent* listed above, Jason Reitman wrote and directed this upbeat story of a twenty-something man just trying to do the right thing by his pet fish. Comedy ensues when he tries to get to the beach to provide him with salt water. The playful plotting includes hilarious twists and turns and an ending that perhaps isn't surprising so much as satisfying.

Hunter And The Swan Discuss Their Meeting (2011); eight minutes

The film was an official selection for the 2011 Sundance Film Festival, Third Place at the 2012 First Run Festival, Winner of a 2012 Student Grant at the USA National Board of Review, and Winner of the Festival Prize at the 2012 Seattle Science-Fiction Short Film Festival.

Written and directed by Emily Carmichael, this short film was made as her thesis film at the NYU graduate film program. The logline on IMDb sums up the story as "A Brooklyn couple has dinner with a hunter and his girlfriend, a magical swan woman. It doesn't go well."[7] And the story that unfolds is both hilarious and sad as we watch a couple implode. What works so well in this story is its theme and the idea that love at first sight isn't necessary for a lasting love relationship.

I Love Sarah Jane (2008); fourteen minutes

The film was an official selection at thirteen film festivals including the 2008 Sundance Film Festival. It won best narrative at four festivals including Arizona, Clermont-Ferrand, Nashville, and Melbourne.

Written and directed by Spencer Susser and co-written by David Michod, *I Love Sarah Jane* is a zombie horror film, but what sets it apart is at its core, it's a coming-of-age love story. It's more than just a gruesome, blowing up and killing zombies story—although there's also plenty of that too. Structurally and thematically, the film has a lot going for it. It has a strong inciting incident, midpoint and end of Act Two. Spencer Susser is a music video director and his feature film debut, *Hesher,* was selected for the 2010 Sundance Film Festival. Mia Wasikowska, the actress who played Jane, went on to star in Tim Burton's *Alice in Wonderland, The Kids Are All Right, Jane Eyre,* and other films.

Inja/Dog (2002); fourteen minutes

Nominated for 2003 Academy Award Best Live Action Short Film, winner of 2002 Best Student Film at Aspen Shortsfest, Second Place Winner at 2001 Palm Springs International Short Fest.

Written and directed by Steve Pasvolsky, *Inja* was his final film made while he was at the Australian Film, Television, and Radio School.[8] The story is about the relationship between dogs and humans and takes place during two time periods in South Africa. The movie opens in colonized South Africa where a white landowner forces his young black worker to abuse a puppy to ensure that the dog favors the white man. Years later, when apartheid was coming to an end, we see this action have surprising consequences. *Inja* is thematically rich as it explores the long-term effects of apartheid in South Africa.

Inside (2002); five minutes

Winner of Best Short Film at 2002 San Diego Film Festival and 2002 San Francisco International Film Festival.

Written and directed by Trevor Sands, *Inside* is a provocative story about multiple personalities. It's a great film to watch for character archetypes as so many are displayed including the orphan, the fool, the caregiver, the sage, the ruler, and the warrior. It also has an incredible surprise ending that few viewers anticipate the first time.

Lights Out (2013); three minutes

Written and directed by David Sandberg and starring his wife, Lotta Losten, this short horror film delivers "jump out of your seat" moments. The story is simple, but scary. Each time a woman turns off her bedside light, she sees a scary figure which causes her to immediately turn the light back on. And each time she sees the figure it gets closer and closer. As stated in the earlier chapter, this short became a great proof of concept for the creators as they went on to make a feature film version in 2016. This short film also shows what can be done with one location, no dialogue, and one character.

Lunch Date (1990); twelve minutes

Winner of 1991 Academy Award for Best Live Action Short Film, 1990 Short Film Palme d'Or at Cannes Film Festival, selected for "Dramatic Achievement" in the 1990 Student Academy Awards, and more recently, the film was selected in 2013 for preservation in the United States National Film Registry by the Library of Congress as being "culturally, historically, or aesthetically significant."[9]

Written and directed by Adam Davidson for his thesis film at the Columbia University graduate program, *Lunch Date* tells the story of a rich white woman who shares her lunch with a black man that she assumes is homeless. Davidson went on to direct successful television shows including *Community, Lost, Deadwood, Grey's Anatomy, Six Feet Under,* and *Fringe. Lunch Date* tells its story almost entirely through visuals. Thematically it's also particularly strong with its "don't judge a book by its cover" message.

Miracle Fish (2009); seventeen minutes

Nominated for the 2010 Academy Award Best Short Film Live Action, winner at twelve film festivals including 2009 Aspen Shortsfest.

Written and directed by Luke Doolan, *Miracle Fish* is about a lonely school boy who is suddenly left all alone at his elementary school only to be faced with a dangerous shooter. Thematically this short shows the power of kindness. *Miracle Fish* not only has a great theme, it also has wonderful plants and payoffs that make us eager to watch the movie over and over. It's also a great film to break down in terms of its structure.

My First Haircut (1988); seven minutes

First Place Winner at the HBO Arts and Entertainment Shorts Festival.

Written and directed by Alex Zamm, *My First Haircut* is literally the story of a little boy's first haircut and shown through his eyes—it is terrifying! It's a great example of a simple story told well. The zinger ending is an added treat. Alex Zamm went on to direct the soon to be released *Woody Woodpecker, Inspector Gadget 2, Chairman of The Board, My Date with the President's Daughter,* and numerous TV films.

Oppressed Majority (2010); eleven minutes

Winner of the Best Short Fiction Film at the 2010 Molodist International Film Festival.

Written and directed by Eleonore Pourriat, *Oppressed Majority* is about a world run by women and imagines how a man might experience sexual assault in a matriarchal society.[10] While the film was made in 2010, it went unnoticed except for a festival award in Kiev. Back in 2010, the feminist fight felt out of date. But then five years later, Pourriat uploaded the film to YouTube and it quickly went viral, picking up over 3 million viewers. Why the sudden interest? Pourriat believed that it was because in 2014, the feminist rights around the world were much more in danger.[11] It's a terrific film for turning the tables on current gender roles in society. Hilarious at times, its themes of class, bigotry, racism, and misogyny resonate throughout.

Plot Device (2011); nine minutes

As described by IMDb, *Plot Device* tells the story of a young filmmaker who obtains a mysterious device that unleashes the full force of cinema on his front lawn.

Written and directed by Seth Worley and co-written by Aharon Rabinowitz, *Plot Device* is a perfect film to watch when learning about film genres as we see the hero jump from a romantic comedy to an action buddy cop genre to a noir to an indie to a sci-fi to animation.

Saturday Night Life (2006); twelve minutes

Before she went on to direct the award-winning *Selma*, Ava duVernay wrote and directed this short drama about a poor, struggling single mother whose trip with her three children to a 99-cent store in Los Angeles becomes an unexpectedly uplifting family experience.[12] When she made the film, duVernay was a publicist and didn't have time or money to stop her career to attend film school. So she took $6,000 and figured things out while in the process of filming.[13] This film is not only a good character study, but the plot takes surprising twists and turns.

Soulmates (2015); one minute

Selected for the 2015 Sundance Film Festival.

Written and directed by Hollywood actress Bryce Dallas Howard, this short film tells the story of a girl and a boy and follows their courtship to her death. But we only see their shoes! And it's all told visually. *Style* magazine also called it an "adorable sixty second love letter to shoes."[14] This is a powerful film even though it's so short. And by the ending, we can't help but tear up.

Strangers (2003); seven minutes

Written and directed by Guy Nattiv and Erez Tadmor, *Strangers* is about two strangers who meet on a train. One is a Jewish man and the other is an Arabic man. In the beginning of this film, the men feel hostility toward each other. But by the end, they bond over a common enemy. This is an excellent film to watch for both its visual storytelling, because there is no dialogue, and for its character transformation. Thematically, the film is also very rich as it suggests we can be friends with our enemies if only we get to know them better.

The Apocalypse (2013); six minutes

Written and directed by Andrew Zuchero, this comedy short is about four friends hanging out and trying to figure out what to do. After the first shock of seeing someone's head blow up, the film gets funnier and funnier. Thematically it is able to visualize the message that having a thought in your head will cause your head to explode because that's exactly what happens.

This is John (2003); eight minutes

Written by Mark Duplass and directed by his brother Jay, this is the film that launched their careers and made them into indie darlings at Sundance and beyond. According to the Internet site Fandor, *This is John* is about "John Ashford, a man with an answering machine and no messages. He figures his outgoing message is to blame so he starts recording a better one. A savvier, sexier, more confident representation of John. That kind of pressure could kill a man."[15] The simplicity of the film makes it worth watching.

Validation (2007); sixteen minutes

Winner of Best Live Action Short Film at the 2007 Cleveland International Film Festival, and the Audience Award at the 2007 Hawaii International Film Festival.

Written and directed by Kurt Kuenn, this is a charming story about a happy-go-lucky parking attendant who likes to give compliments to everyone while he validates their parking ticket. Why? Because he loves to see people smile. Trouble ensues when he compliments a young woman and he can't make her smile.

Zen And The Art Of Landscaping (2001); seventeen minutes

Winner of the 2001 Student Academy Award for Narrative Film. Honorable Mention for Short Filmmaking at 2001 Sundance Film Festival. Jury Award at 2001 Aspen Shortsfest. And awards at numerous other festivals including Boston Underground, Rehoboth Beach, and Deauville.

Written and directed by David Kartch for his thesis film at Columbia University. The Aspen Shortsfest describes the film as, "A beautifully orchestrated, impeccably timed, escalating series of twists, revelations and surprises in a hilarious landscape where only a weed-whacker can afford protection."[16]

ENDNOTES

1. http://curfewfilm.com/awards/

2. http://www.openculture.com/2013/10/christopher-nolans-first-short-doodlebug.html

3. http://www.indiewire.com/2016/08/duffer-brothers-short-film-eater-stranger-things-directors-1201713815/

4. http://www.imdb.com/title/tt1631323/awards?ref_=tt_awd

5. http://www.imdb.com/title/tt1631323/

6. http://www.imdb.com/title/tt0281850/awards?ref_=tt_awd

7. http://www.imdb.com/title/tt1715218/

8. https://de.wikipedia.org/wiki/Steve_Pasvolsky

9. https://en.wikipedia.org/wiki/The_Lunch_Date

10. http://www.imdb.com/title/tt1684911/news

11. https://www.theguardian.com/lifeandstyle/womens-blog/2014/feb/11/oppressed-majority-film-women-eleonore-pourriat

12. http://www.sho.com/titles/129593/black-filmmaker-showcase-saturday-night-life

13. http://filmmakermagazine.com/57145-love-on-the-outside/#.V_qq5dxQJyc

14. instyle.com/news/watch-bryce-dallas-howard-60-second-love-letter-shoes

15. https://www.fandor.com/films/this_is_john

16. http://www.imdb.com/title/tt0247836/awards?ref_=tt_awd

SHORT FILMS TO WATCH

We've given you a great list of short films to watch but for every film we've listed there are hundreds of other terrific short films. Go on the Internet and look for other films that you like. Consider looking at "short of the week" for Tribeca or Sundance, or Academy Award shorts. Or just put the words "short films" in the search engine and see what comes up. Then watch the films.

In the space below, keep a list of all the short films you've watched.

TITLE	FILMMAKER	RUNNING TIME

CHAPTER 14

Proof of Concept Exercises

The exercises listed on the following pages are intended for the indicated chapters. Our hope is that after you read a particular chapter, you will do the corresponding exercise. This will put you on a positive path of writing.

EXERCISE #1—LEARNING TO WRITE VISUALLY

After you read Chapter 2 on Visual Storytelling, do the following exercise.

Write a ONE-page scene using the following prompt:

> **Show us the moment when one character catches another character cheating.**

This doesn't have to be a romantic scene. In fact it's better if it's more creative than that. Think of the many arenas where characters can cheat: school, sports, work, church. A casino. A locker room bathroom.

EXERCISE #2—LEARNING TO WRITE GREAT DIALOGUE

After you read Chapter 3 on Dialogue, do the following exercise.

Using ONLY DIALOGUE, write a three-page scene about the stressful breakup of some sort of relationship. Breakups can be:

- ► Romantic
- ► Work-related
- ► Family-related
- ► School-related

Any situation that might involve a breakup!

If you're stuck for a beginning, start with the line "I got your text."

Create two characters with distinctive and different styles of speech. See how much information you can convey through what they're not saying using subtext.

Don't be ordinary. Don't be boring.

> Girl dumping boy is boring. President dumping Vice President is interesting. Girl dumping boy is interesting, if she's doing it while they're performing surgery.

No descriptions! No parentheticals! Nothing but dialogue. But it's okay to use a scene heading.

EXERCISE #3—BUILD A PROTAGONIST

After you've read Chapter 4 on Crafting Characters, do the following exercise for the protagonist of your short film.

1. What is the NAME of this character?

2. What is his/her SEX? What is the AGE?

3. Describe their APPEARANCE.

4. What is the OCCUPATION or MAJOR of this character?

5. What are this character's AMUSEMENTS? HOBBIES?

6. What is this character's GHOST or INTERNAL PROBLEM?

7. What is this character's POLE-TO-POLE TRANSFORMATION?

8. Is this character an INTROVERT? EXTROVERT?

9. What are this character's STRENGTHS AND VIRTUES?

10. What are this character's FAULTS AND WEAKNESSES?

11. What class in SOCIETY does this character belong to?

12. What type of EDUCATION has the character had?

13. What type of HOME LIFE does this character have?

14. What type of LOVE LIFE or SEX LIFE does this character have?

15. What is this character's PERSONAL AMBITION?

16. What are the character's FRUSTRATIONS? CHIEF LIFE DISAPPOINTMENTS?

17. What are the character's DREAMS in life—both childhood and current?

18. What are this character's COMPLEXITIES? OBSESSIONS? SUPERSTITIONS? PHOBIAS?

19. What is this character's RACE? NATIONALITY?

20. What is this character's PLACE IN THE COMMUNITY?

21. What are this character's POLITICS?

22. What is this character's RELIGION?

23. What is this character's EXTERNAL PROBLEM?

EXERCISE #4—ELEVATOR CHARACTER SCENE

After you've read Chapter 4, here's the exercise for writing distinctive characters.

In five pages, write a scene using the following prompt:

> No one wants to be stuck in an elevator. They just don't!
> Now imagine being stuck with your FAMILY in an elevator!
> Everyone wants the same thing—TO GET OUT OF THE ELEVATOR.
> Why? Are they claustrophobic? Do they have someplace else to be? Can they not stand being with each other?
> It's up to you.

Create a family of FOUR PEOPLE using the FOUR ELEMENTS (earth, wind, fire, and water) and put them in an elevator.

> Have them all going somewhere together. It can be anything from a wedding, to a funeral, to a doctor's appointment, to a reunion. You decide where they're going.
> Then, what happens next?
> The conflict is going to come out of character. Who emerges as the leader?
> What is the plan of action?

NUMBER ONE RULE: They can't all agree with each other. Alliances can be formed. But there needs to be disagreement.

EXERCISE #5—SCENE EXERCISE: GLAD I BUMPED INTO YOU . . . OR NOT?

After you've read Chapter 5 on Writing the Scene, do the following exercise.
Here's the prompt: write a four-page scene using the following rules:

Two characters bump into each other and they are forced to deal with each other.
It could be at a . . .

- ► Car accident
- ► Bank robbery
- ► Restaurant
- ► Hospital
- ► A location of your choosing

The important thing is that they are both right.
There is no villain here—only conflicting interests.

Example: Let's say our two characters are a thirty-something man and a thirty-something pregnant woman. If they bumped into each other at the hospital the dialogue could be, "So what's it been? Nine months?" And suddenly we learn that Gary disappeared because he was kidnapped while working for Doctors without Borders. And then Jackie, the pregnant mom, has him do a paternity test. We hope he's the dad. Then we learn he's not. Disappointment. She leaves. Alone.

EXERCISE #6—LOGLINE WORKSHEET

After you've read Chapter 7 on What to Write, Why to Write? do the following exercise on creating a logline for your ten-to fifteen-page short film.

In the TONE of _____
               (a successful movie which made lots of money)

_____

(your TITLE)

is a _____
(GENRE)

about _____
(PROTAGONIST—CHARACTER)

who is _____
(STATUS QUO—living his/her life—whatever that is for your character)

when _____
(SOMETHING HAPPENS)

and he/she must do _____
(to achieve their GOAL)

or else _____
(some kind of disaster will happen if he/she doesn't succeed)

EXERCISE #7—NOTES FOR A REWRITE

After reading Chapter 10, use this form to critique your script or a friend's script.

1. CONFLICT
   Is there conflict in every scene?
   Point out where conflict is lacking.

2. PACING
   Are the scenes about two to three pages or do they drag on too long?
   Is the inciting incident occurring early enough in the script?

3. CHARACTERS
   Are the characters introduced in an interesting way?
   Are the characters distinctive from each other?

4. DIALOGUE
   Indicate where it's too on the nose and where there's subtext.
   Indicate where it's good.

5. THEME
   What is the theme of this short script?

6. THE RESOLUTION
   Is there a zinger ending?
   Is the ending satisfying? If not, what could the ending be?

7. OVERALL IMPRESSIONS
   What is working? What isn't working?

CPSIA information can be obtained
at www.ICGtesting.com
Printed in the USA
LVHW062317291119
638458LV00005B/6/P